Unleash the Power of Customer Engagement & Advocacy

Practical guide towards customer advocacy incl. end-to-end cookbook for successful Customer Advisory Boards

Timo Wagenblatt

Unleash the Power of Customer Engagement & Advocacy

Copyright © 2024 Timo Wagenblatt

No part of this book may be reproduced, or stored in a retrieval system, or transmitted in any form or by any means, electronic, mechanical, photocopying, recording, or otherwise, without express written permission of the publisher.

All rights reserved.

ISBN-13: 9798326076076

Imprint: Independently published

CONTENT

PREFACE I

I. HOLISTIC PRODUCT MANAGEMENT: THE KEY TO UNLOCKING YOUR PRODUCT'S FULL POTENTIAL 13

    Introduction..13

    What is Holistic Product Management?...13

    Why It Matters - The High Costs of Product Waste...............................13

    The PYPR Framework 14

    Benefits of Holistic Product Management (and PYPRing your Product) 16

    Customer Engagement & Advocacy Impact on Product Success 16

    The Bottom Line 17

1 THE CUSTOMER CONNECTION: WHY ENGAGEMENT AND ADVOCACY ARE THE HEART OF YOUR BUSINESS 18

    Introduction..18

    Defining Customer Engagement & Advocacy......................................19

    The Flywheel Effect: A Virtuous Cycle 20

    The Power of the Engaged and Vocal Customer 22

    A Success Story: Miro's Rise Fueled by Advocacy..............................22

    A Glimpse at the Business Case for Customer Advocacy....................22

    Key Takeaways 23

    Time for Action 23

2 THE SPECTRUM OF CUSTOMER ENGAGEMENT: PATHWAYS TO ADVOCACY ...24

    Introduction..24

    Personalized Interactions 24

    Content-Driven Engagement 25

    Community Engagement 25

    Event-Based Engagement 26

    Feedback and Co-Creation 26

Case Study: Steering a Customer Advisory Board with Product Vision and Commitment 27
- *Context* *27*
- *Situation* *27*
- *Response and Leadership* *27*
- *Resolution and Co-Innovation* *28*
- *Outcome* *28*
- *Lessons Learned* *29*

B2B vs. B2C Environment Considerations 29

The Power of Choice: Building Your Engagement Mix 30

Summary and Key Takeaways 30

Time for Action: Empowering Product Managers with an Integrated Engagement Blueprint 31
- *The Role of the Product Manager* *31*
- *Importance of a Coordinated Team Effort* *31*
- *Practical Application: Not Boiling the Ocean* *31*

3 THE CUSTOMER ADVOCACY PYRAMID – A COMPREHENSIVE FRAMEWORK FOR SUCCESS 33

Introduction 33

Components of the Customer Advocacy Pyramid 34

Benefit of CABs 35

Key Characteristics of Effective CABs 36

Executive and Customer Advisory Boards – A Comparison 37

The Role of Product Management 38

Recruiting CAB Customer Candidates 38

Structuring the CAB Planning and Execution Team 39
- *Key Roles for Effective CABs and the Customer Advocacy Pyramid* *39*

The Flywheel in Action 41

Success Story: Harnessing Customer Engagement at SAP 41
- *Introduction* *41*
- *Building the Foundation with CPAC* *42*
- *Expanding the Engagement: CABs and Co-Innovation* *42*

    The Flywheel in Action *42*
    Showcasing Success: SAPPHIRE and Beyond *43*
    A Model of Integrated Strategy *44*

The Role of Product 44

B2B vs. B2C Environment Considerations 45

Connecting It All Together 45

4 THE CUSTOMER ADVISORY BOARD COOKBOOK **47**

Introduction 47

Step-by-Step Guide for Effective Customer Advisory Boards 48
    Step 1: Evaluate the Need for Customer Advisory Boards *49*
    Step 2: Plan Customer Advisory Boards *52*
    Step 2a: Initial Setup and Team Engagement *52*
    Step 2b: CAB Project Plan including Scheduling and Financial Planning *53*
    Step 2c: Customer Advisory Council Communications Approach *57*
    Step 3: Execute Customer Advisory Boards *61*
    Step 4: Follow-up on Customer Advisory Boards *64*
    Step 5: Leverage Customer Advisory Boards for Product Success *66*

Summary and Key Takeaways 69

Customer Advisory Board (CAB) Project Plan (Template) 71
    Project Plan Overview *71*
    Task Breakdown *72*

CAB Agenda Template, Best Practices, and Examples 75
    Core Agenda Components *75*
    Additional Agenda Options *76*
    Illustrative 2-Day CAB Agenda Template *77*
    Best Practices *78*
    Example Agenda: First CAB Meeting for Single Product *79*
    Example Agenda: Established CAB for Product Line *80*

Templates: Communication Types and Best Practices 81
    Save the Date Invitation Template *81*
    Invite to Collaboration Group Template *82*
    CAB Membership Invitation Template *83*
    CAB Meeting Invitation Template *84*

5 COMPLETING THE CUSTOMER ADVOCACY PYRAMID 85

Introduction 85
Establishing Co-Innovation Workstreams 85
    Structure and Functioning 86
    Benefits 87
User Groups, Communities, and Meet-Ups 87
Lights on – Showcase Customer Engagement and Advocacy 90
B2B vs. B2C Environment Considerations 91
Key Takeaways 91

6 AMPLIFYING PRODUCT SUCCESS THROUGH CUSTOMER REFERENCES AND TESTIMONIALS 93

Introduction 93
The Strategic Importance of Customer References 93
Leveraging CABs for Dynamic Customer References 94
Structuring Your Customer Reference Approach 95
Integrating or Establishing Customer Loyalty Programs 96
Utilizing Customer References 97
Key Takeaways for Effective Customer Reference Management 98
    Structured Reference Process 98
    Quality Over Quantity 98
    Strategic Use of References 98
    Timing and Necessity 98
    Empower Your Teams 99
    The Power of Saying No 99

7 MEASURING SUCCESS ACROSS THE CUSTOMER ADVOCACY PYRAMID 100

Introduction 100
Establishing Comprehensive Success Metrics 100
Implementing the Measurement Process 102
Leveraging CABs and Community Engagement for Powerful Customer References 103
Conclusion 103

8 HARNESSING THE POWER OF CUSTOMER PERSONALITIES ACROSS ENGAGEMENT PLATFORMS 105

    Introduction..105

    Identifying Customer Personalities 105

    Engaging Personalities in Different Formats 106

        Executive Advisory Boards (EABs) 106

        Customer Advisory Boards (CABs) 106

        Co-Innovation Workstreams 106

        User Groups, Communities, and Meet-Ups 106

        Customer References/Testimonials 107

    Conclusion 107

    Key Takeaways 107

9 CUSTOMER ENGAGEMENT & ADVOCACY AS PART OF THE PYPR FRAMEWORK FOR SUSTAINABLE PRODUCT SUCCESS..108

    Introduction..108

    The Positive Cross-effects of Unleashing the Power of Customer Engagement & Advocacy...108

    The Role of Advocacy in Amplifying Impact 111

    Conclusion 111

    Explore More Resources...111

ABOUT THE AUTHOR 113

REFERENCES 114

FIGURES 115

Preface

Welcome to "Unleash the Power of Customer Engagement & Advocacy," a pivotal installment in the Product&360 Nuggets Series. This series is designed to support CPOs, founders, product leads, product teams, and product managers in achieving peak performance through Holistic Product Management. Our mission is clear: to minimize product waste and transform promising product potentials into remarkable successes.

In a market flooded with underperforming products, our transformative experience unlocks the true potential of your products, teams, leadership, and organizations. The Product Yield Potential Radar (PYPR) approach, central to our methodology, is a framework to help you visualize and manage the 360-degree view of your products and product organization.

This book is crafted for those who sense that their products, teams, and personal efforts deserve greater recognition and success. It offers a comprehensive perspective that goes beyond traditional product management by integrating customer insights, market dynamics, and organizational structure into a cohesive strategy.

Who Should Read This Book

"Unleash the Power of Customer Engagement & Advocacy" is an essential resource for:

- Emerging and seasoned product leaders ready to take customer-centricity to the next level.

- Product marketing managers looking to align deeper market insights with actionable strategies.

- Customer success enthusiasts eager to drive sustainable customer satisfaction and advocacy.

- Event planners focused on crafting memorable and impactful customer experiences.

Through this book, you will learn how to harness the full spectrum of customer engagement—from the foundational Customer Advisory Boards to dynamic co-innovation workstreams—and transform these elements into a powerful advocacy network that propels your product to market leadership.

How This Book Is Organized

The organization of the content is designed to guide you through a logical progression of enhancing customer engagement and leveraging it for product and organizational success:

1. **Holistic Product Management**: Introduces the Product&360 approach and PYPR – a framework to help you visualize and manage the 360-degree view of your products and product organization.

2. **The Customer Connection**: Explores the vital role of customer engagement and advocacy in differentiating your product in the marketplace.

3. **The Spectrum of Customer Engagement**: Details various strategies to engage customers, from personalized interactions to community building and beyond.

4. **The Customer Advocacy Pyramid**: Dives into the components that make up a successful customer advocacy strategy, emphasizing the crucial role of CABs.

5. **CAB Cookbook**: Provides a detailed, step-by-step guide to planning, executing, and leveraging Customer Advisory Boards for sustained product success.

6. **Amplifying Product Success Through Customer References and Testimonials**: Shows how to use CAB insights to generate compelling customer references that drive sales and improve market perception.

7. **Measuring Success Across the Customer Advocacy Pyramid**: Discusses how to establish and monitor success metrics that reflect true customer and product engagement.

8. **Harnessing the Power of Customer Personalities Across Engagement Platforms**: Offers insights into identifying and engaging different customer personalities within various engagement contexts.

9. **Customer Engagement & Advocacy as Part of the PYPR Framework for Sustainable Product Success**: Wraps up with a comprehensive look at integrating customer engagement strategies within the broader spectrum of holistic product management.

This book doesn't just narrate theories but empowers you with actionable insights and proven strategies to transform your customer relationships into a growth-driving force.

Get ready to transform your approach, elevate your product, and achieve the success you know you and your team deserve. Let's begin this transformative journey together. Welcome to holistic product management—where your path to peak performance begins.

#BusinessStrategy #CustomerCentricity #Innovation #MarketInsights #Leadership #CustomerAdvisoryBoard #BusinessGrowth

I. Holistic Product Management: The Key to Unlocking Your Product's Full Potential

Introduction

In the world of software products, success isn't about building great shiny features or embedding AI in your offerings. It's about mastering a complex interplay of factors that many product teams overlook. This is where holistic product management comes in – a strategic approach that focuses on long-term, sustainable success.

What is Holistic Product Management?

Think of holistic product management as a 360-degree view of your product. It goes beyond developing and launching features to encompass:

- **Product Viability:** Is your product profitable, valuable, scalable, and easy to implement?
- **Product Development**: Strong vision, planning, execution, and team health.
- **Go-to-Market / Product Marketing:** Effective positioning, messaging, and enablement.
- **The Market / Your Customers:** Understanding needs, experimentation, gathering feedback, and building community.
- **Software Demonstrations and Training:** Clear, compelling showcases of the product's value. Useful learning and training options.
- **Organizational Maturity:** Leadership, processes, and a product success-focused mindset throughout the company.

Why It Matters - The High Costs of Product Waste

Despite the leaps we've made in product – lean methodologies, product discovery, dual track agile, problem focus, AI-powered insights, to name just a few – product waste and failure remain alarmingly high. Startups flame out, promising products fizzle, and even established offerings fall short of their potential. We deliver too much work that doesn't create customer and business value, or we are building something that's rarely used. Rich Mironov called this: Product Waste.

We produce too much product waste and product failures.

Product waste and failure isn't just about the extreme of companies going out of business. It's about the wasted effort, the unrealized value, and the missed opportunities to truly delight customers and drive growth. It's the frustration of knowing your product teams and the whole organization is capable of greatness, yet something's holding you back.

Very often, it's a lack of holistic thinking. We get hyper-focused on one aspect – be it engineering, growth hacking, or the latest tech trend – while neglecting other critical dimensions. This approach creates imbalances that undermine our success.

Imagine building a Ferrari but forgetting the steering wheel. Or crafting a beautiful essay that reaches no one. These scenarios, while extreme, illustrate the point: even excellence in one area can't compensate for neglect elsewhere.

Lack of holistic thinking creates too much product waste and product failures, despite you, the product, and your organization having great pockets of excellence (e.g. technology, biz model or something else).

Why don't you have the success that all the hard work and dedication deserves? You don't know? You can't know, it is not on your radar!

This is where PYPR becomes your strategic advantage.

The PYPR Framework

The Product Yield Potential Radar (PYPR) is a framework to help you visualize and manage the 360-degree view of your product organization.

- **A tool for balance**: Visualizes your product's performance across the 6 dimensions, revealing strengths and weaknesses.
- **Driving focus:** Highlights areas needing attention, preventing overemphasis on any single aspect. Reveals the areas that will have the biggest impact on your product's success.
- **Fostering a product mindset:** Encourages the entire organization to think holistically about product success and how their work contributes towards the best possible outcomes.

By rating your product across all key success factors supported by a proven blueprint of success factors and the criteria to assess each of them, you can pinpoint areas that need attention.

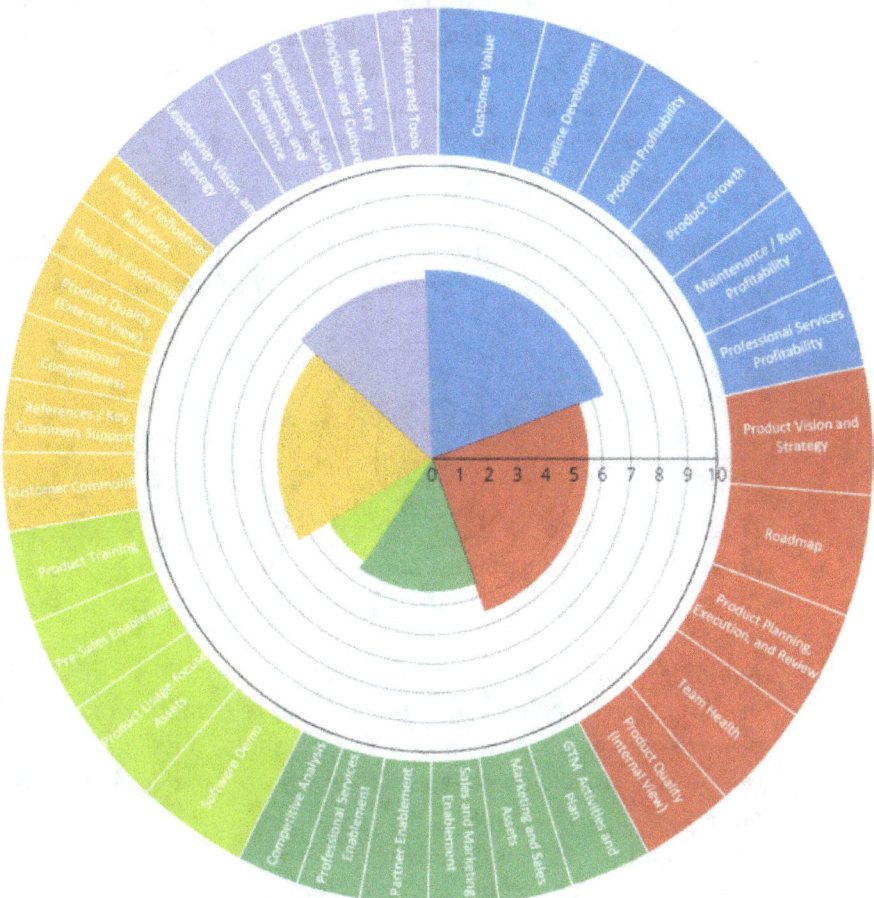

Figure 1: B2B Product PYPR Blueprint

- **Product Viability:** Customer Value, Pipeline Development, Product Profitability, Product Growth, Run Profitability, Professional Services Profitability
- **Product Development**: Product Vision & Strategy, Roadmap, Product Planning, Execution & Review, Team Health, Product Quality (internal view)

- **Go-to-Market / Product Marketing:** GTM activities & plan, Marketing & Sales Assets, Marketing & Sales Enablement, Partner Enablement, Competitive Analysis
- **The Market / Your Customers:** Analyst / Influencer Relations, Thought Leadership, Product Quality (external view), Functional Completeness, References & other Key Customer Support, Customer Community & Advocacy
- **Software Demonstrations and Training:** Product Training, Pre-Sales Enablement, Product-usage based Assets, Software Demonstrations
- **Organizational Maturity:** Leadership Vision & Strategy, Organization Structure, Processes & Portfolio Management, Talent, Culture

Benefits of Holistic Product Management (and PYPRing your Product)

- **True Product-Led Growth:** Understand your product's true potential. It's not just about building features, it's about ensuring the entire organization understands and supports the product's success.
- **Avoiding Wasted Effort:** Focus efforts where they'll have the biggest impact. Spending more time on development won't help if other areas (e.g. poor product marketing, missing customer references, mediocre analyst ratings) are undermining your efforts.
- **Fostering a Product Mindset:** Break down silos and unite cross-functional teams around a common goal. PYPR encourages everyone to think holistically about the product, leading to better decision-making.

Customer Engagement & Advocacy Impact on Product Success

The impact of customer engagement and advocacy extends far beyond individual success stories; it underpins every dimension of holistic product management. By prioritizing customer relationships and turning them into advocates, you create a powerful, self-reinforcing flywheel that fuels growth and resilience. For example,

- **Product Viability**: Customer engagement through CABs and co-innovation workstreams identifies opportunities for increased customer value, pipeline development, and profitability. Satisfied advocates expand market share via positive referrals.

- **Product Development**: CABs and co-innovation groups provide crucial feedback, refining product strategy and planning while beta testing ensures quality and alignment with customer needs.

- **The Market/Your Customers**: Advocates highlight thought leadership, build a strong user community, and enhance positive perceptions among analysts and influencers.

More details can be found in chapter 9 Customer Engagement & Advocacy as part of the PYPR framework for Sustainable Product Success.

This book will guide you through the interconnected processes that align your product team and organization toward holistic success. So, let's dive in and explore how these components come together to maximize your product's potential.

The Bottom Line

Holistic product management is hard, but it's the path to sustainable success. By balancing all aspects of the whole product experience, you maximize your chances of creating products that truly resonate with the market and deliver lasting value.

Holistic product management isn't just a buzzword. It's a proven approach to maximize and fully exploit your product's potential. By embracing it, you'll create products that not only delight customers but also drive real business results.

Want to learn more?

Check out http://www.productand.com or dive into the comprehensive holistic product management (PYPR) book. Your product deserves nothing less than holistic success!

Reading further into "Unleash the Power of Customer Engagement & Advocacy," you'll discover how to implement these strategies across the

Customer Advocacy Pyramid, building the momentum you need to transform satisfied customers into lifelong allies.

1 The Customer Connection: Why Engagement and Advocacy are the Heart of Your Business

Introduction

Imagine a world where your customers don't just use your product—they love it. They rave about it to their friends, colleagues, and online followers. They actively defend your brand when faced with criticism. They provide invaluable insights that shape your product strategy and roadmap.

This isn't a fantasy. It's the reality of companies that have mastered the art of customer engagement and advocacy.

In "Unleash the Power of Customer Engagement & Advocacy", we'll explore the proven strategies and tactics that turn satisfied customers into passionate brand ambassadors.

You'll learn how to build a customer-centric culture, gather and act on valuable feedback, create personalized experiences, foster thriving communities, and establish impactful Customer Advisory Boards.

Whether you're a seasoned product manager, a budding product lead, a driven product marketing manager, a customer success enthusiast, or a customer event planner seeking to create unforgettable customer experiences, this book will equip you with the tools and knowledge you need to drive customer loyalty, innovation, and sustainable growth.

In today's crowded marketplace, true differentiation comes from how you connect with your customers – whether you sell a B2C app or a complex B2B enterprise solution. The companies that build lasting success understand that true differentiation lies in the relationships they build with their customers. This isn't about a fluffy "customer-centric" buzzword – this is about understanding that engaged customers and passionate advocates are the key to unlocking growth, innovation, and resilience.

The companies that truly succeed are those that don't simply sell a product or service – they build relationships. They turn customers into champions. Satisfied customers are great, but advocates are the lifeblood of any product-led business. Customer engagement and advocacy are the secret ingredients to success.

Get ready to transform your customers into your most powerful allies.

The journey starts here. =>>

Defining Customer Engagement & Advocacy

Let's clarify these core terms, considering both B2C and B2B contexts:

- **Customer Engagement**: At its heart, engagement means building ongoing relationships. Think of it as the heartbeat of your relationship with your customers. Engagement is a genuine, ongoing conversation. It's listening to feedback, responding to questions, providing educational content, and creating a sense of belonging around your product, brand, or company. Customers feel valued and heard.
    - **B2C:** Think personalized recommendations on your favorite e-commerce site, social media contests, or loyalty programs that make you feel valued.
    - **B2B:** Think webinars tailored to specific industries, user groups addressing common challenges, or personalized onboarding for new clients.

- **Customer Advocacy:** This is where the magic happens. Advocacy takes engagement to the next level. Advocates aren't just satisfied customers; they are your most enthusiastic supporters. Advocates are those customers who are not only loyal but who actively promote your product or service to others. They share their positive experiences, write testimonials, provide valuable referrals, participate in case studies, recommend your product to their professional networks, and genuinely want to see you succeed. Think of them as an unpaid extension of your sales and marketing teams!
    - **B2C Environments:** Advocates generate social buzz with product reviews, unboxing videos, or enthusiastic recommendations to their friends and family.
    - **B2B Environments:** Advocates may write case studies, speak at industry events, provide referrals, or collaborate on product roadmaps with your team.

The distinction between engagement and advocacy is crucial. While the former focuses on maintaining and deepening relationships, the latter transforms these relationships into active promotion and endorsement of your product, brand, and company.

The Flywheel Effect: A Virtuous Cycle

Customer advocacy isn't a one-time initiative, it's a self-reinforcing process. When you invest in customer engagement and deliver on your promises, you increase customer satisfaction. Satisfied customers are more likely to become advocates. Advocates attract more customers with their satisfaction and enthusiasm. And the cycle continues!

Figure 2: The Engagement-Advocacy Flywheel

Regardless of your business model, the concept of engagement driving advocacy driving growth is universal. However, the flywheel turns in slightly different ways for different contexts:

- **B2C Environment:** Momentum may build rapidly through social sharing, but individual advocacy impact is often lower due to smaller purchase amounts. Volume is crucial.

- **B2B Environments:** Momentum is often slower, but long-term, high-value clients can make a massive impact with a few positive references or case studies. Focus on depth of advocacy.

The impact of genuine engagement and advocacy extends far beyond a few good testimonials. Consider tech giants like Salesforce, SAP, and Atlassian. These companies didn't achieve market dominance solely through product superiority. Their vibrant user communities, filled with passionate advocates, have propelled them forward, acting as an organic force of market awareness, lead generation, and innovation. Engaged customers and advocates provide:

- **Trust & Social Proof**: Word-of-mouth recommendations and authentic case studies are more convincing than any ad campaign.
- **A Competitive Edge**: A loyal, vocal customer base creates a barrier for competitors – why switch if you love your current solution and trust the people behind it?
- **Product Insights**: Engaged customers provide invaluable, unfiltered feedback. This fuels iterations and drives continuous improvement.
- **Reduced Marketing Spend**: When your customers are your best marketers, traditional acquisition channels are supported by strong tailwinds.

While the basic benefits remain true, their emphasis might shift taking the product context into consideration:

B2C Environment:

- **Trust & Social Proof:** Vital in a market where consumers are inundated with choices.
- **Rapid Product Insights:** Social media buzz and reviews provide immediate feedback on new features or promotions.
- **Virality:** User-generated content fuels growth at minimal cost.

B2B Environment:

- **Thought leadership:** Customer success stories establish your expertise.

- **Long-term Relationships**: Advocacy builds trust, critical in high-consideration sales cycles.
- **Reduced Churn:** Strong client relationships prevent switching for cheaper alternatives.

The Power of the Engaged and Vocal Customer

Don't underestimate the ripple effects of turning customers into fans. Consider the meteoric rise of companies like Figma, Zoom, and Slack. Yes, they offer fantastic products, but their exponential growth has been fueled by the passion of their user bases. Engaged customers and advocates become your company's secret weapon. They:

- **Boost Brand Awareness:** Testimonials and case studies resonate more deeply than any ad campaign ever could.
- **Drive Lead Generation:** Referrals from trusted sources are incredibly valuable leads.
- **Increase Product Adoption:** Advocates can help onboard new users, troubleshoot problems, and suggest new features.
- **Provide Invaluable Feedback:** Engaged customers tell you what they love and what needs fixing. This insight is pure gold for product strategy and development.

A Success Story: Miro's Rise Fueled by Advocacy

Miro, the online whiteboard platform, provides a fantastic case study. They've embraced customer engagement from day one. Through community forums, webinars, and a focus on customer education, they've built a loyal following. This user base became their greatest asset, with advocates eagerly sharing Miro with their colleagues, sparking viral adoption across teams and even entire companies. (Meabe, 2024)

A Glimpse at the Business Case for Customer Advocacy

While building great customer relationships feels good, it directly impacts your bottom line. Investing in engagement and advocacy leads to:

- **Reduced Customer Acquisition Costs (CAC):** Happy customers become your marketing engine, reducing the expense of traditional channels.

Advocacy-driven leads are less expensive to acquire and convert at a higher rate. B2C advocates lower acquisition costs through viral content or by becoming affiliates. Engagement boosts lifetime value through increased purchasing frequency. B2B advocacy drives leads within niche markets. Engaged customers drive upgrades and expansions, boosting revenue with existing accounts.

- **Increased Customer Lifetime Value (CLV):** Engaged customers churn less, upgrade more frequently, and have lower churn rates plus tend to expand their usage over time.
- **Improved Product-Market Fit:** Advocates provide a goldmine of honest feedback, ensuring your product truly meets their needs and making your product even stronger.
- **Boosted Company Valuation:** Businesses with a strong track record of advocacy often command higher valuations, a vital consideration for potential investors or acquirers.

Key Takeaways

- ✓ Customer engagement and advocacy are essential for business success in the modern world.
- ✓ Engagement and advocacy are tailored strategies, yet both are essential for B2C and B2B success.
- ✓ Customer advocacy transforms your best customers into your biggest cheerleaders.
- ✓ Advocates provide social proof and build trust, vital for any sales process.
- ✓ There's a clear ROI tied to customer advocacy, impacting acquisition costs, revenue, and overall value.
- ✓ Advocacy fuels organic growth – from viral content to high-value referrals.

Time for Action

Understanding the 'why' of customer engagement and advocacy is crucial, but it's the 'how' that matters. In the coming chapters, we'll get tactical. We'll explore strategies tailored to your context for fostering engagement, developing an army of advocates, and building a customer-centric culture that propels your business forward.

2 The Spectrum of Customer Engagement: Pathways to Advocacy

Introduction

In Chapter 1, we explored the transformative power of customer engagement and advocacy. Now, let's delve deeper and discover the various ways to cultivate these valuable relationships. Just like a prism refracts light into a spectrum of colors, customer engagement encompasses a range of interactions, each playing a vital role in the journey towards brand advocacy.

Engagement is not a one-size-fits-all approach. Different types of customer engagement cater to varying aspects of the customer journey and business model, each with its unique set of strategies, benefits, and challenges.

In this chapter, we explore five distinct types of customer engagement, providing detailed insights into how each can be harnessed to cultivate strong customer advocates. From direct interactions to leveraging digital platforms, understanding these modalities will help you craft an engagement strategy that not only resonates with your customers but also turns them into your most vocal supporters.

Personalized Interactions

Personalized interactions involve tailoring communication and experiences to fit the individual needs and preferences of each customer. This can include customized emails, product recommendations, streamlined buying processes, offering user-friendly interfaces, and providing efficient customer support channels (phone, chat, email, and one-on-one support).

This is the foundation of the customer relationship. It involves the core interactions a customer has when purchasing, using, or receiving support for your product or service.

Benefits: Creates a positive first impression, builds trust, and establishes a baseline for future interactions. Personalized engagement fosters a deeper emotional connection, enhancing customer satisfaction and loyalty. It makes customers feel valued and understood, which are key drivers of advocacy.

Challenges: The main challenge lies in scaling personalized interactions without compromising the quality or personal touch. It requires robust data analytics and integration across platforms to maintain consistency and relevance. Scaling personalized interactions can feel impersonal, and repetitive interactions without additional engagement can lead to customer churn.

Content-Driven Engagement

Providing valuable and informative content tailored to customer interests and industry trends. Move beyond simple transactions and provide customers with valuable knowledge and resources. This includes blogs, whitepapers, videos, educational content, tutorials, webinars, or customer success stories, knowledge base or FAQ section, and infographics that educate and engage the customer base.

Benefits: Content-driven engagement establishes thought leadership and trust. It helps in educating customers, thereby enhancing their ability to use and advocate for the product more effectively. Content-driven engagement empowers customers, reduces support inquiries, and positions your product and organization as a thought leader.

Challenges: The key challenge is consistently producing high-quality content that stands out in an oversaturated market. It requires ongoing content creation and ensuring information is up-to-date and readily accessible. Additionally, linking content engagement directly to sales can be indirect and complex.

Community Engagement

This type of engagement builds communities around a brand, product, or service, either online or offline. Communities foster a sense of belonging. It includes forums, user groups, and social media communities creating spaces where customers can interact with each other around your product and with your brand and company. Facilitate or encourage the formation of both in-person and online community formats focused on your product or service. Provide resources, seed topics for discussion, and consider offering moderation for both official and self-organized groups.

Benefits: Community engagement boosts customer retention and loyalty by creating a sense of belonging. It provides a platform for peer support and shared learning, which can enhance product usage and satisfaction.

Challenges: Managing a community requires continuous moderation and content generation. It requires active community management to ensure a positive and inclusive environment. It also poses risks of negative feedback spreading quickly if customer concerns are not addressed promptly.

Event-Based Engagement

Hosting or participating in events such as webinars, workshops, conferences, and seminars. These events can be in-person or virtual, providing direct engagement opportunities. Consider your participation in relevant industry trade shows and conferences (e.g. sponsor events, secure speaking opportunities, have a well-designed booth to attract engagement) and network with key decision-makers and potential customers.

Benefits: Events can create memorable experiences that strengthen brand affinity and knowledge. They also offer networking opportunities that can lead to stronger business relationships and advocacy.

Challenges: Events demand significant planning and resources. Measuring ROI can be challenging, and the impact may vary widely based on the event's execution and relevance to the audience.

Feedback and Co-Creation

Take engagement a step further by encouraging active participation and feedback from customers. Engaging customers through feedback surveys, focus groups, and involving them in the product development process via beta testing or co-creation workshops.

Benefits: This engagement type directly informs product improvements and innovations, ensuring that the offerings align closely with customer needs. It makes customers feel directly involved in the product journey, fostering a strong sense of ownership and advocacy.

Challenges: It requires a structured approach to gathering, analyzing, and acting on feedback. There is also the challenge of managing diverse opinions and ensuring that participants do not feel overlooked if their suggestions are not implemented. Do not overcommit yourself to delivering what your customers are asking for. A clear "No", or "Yes, but not now" is superior to a "Yes" that will not be delivered.

Case Study: Steering a Customer Advisory Board with Product Vision and Commitment

Context

As a Product Lead for a leading Customer Business Planning software used by top Consumer Packaged Goods (CPG) companies such as Mondelez, Red Bull, PepsiCo, Henkel, The Coca Cola Company, Nestlé, Johnsonville Sausages, Florida Crystals, and Unilever just to name a few of the 30, you oversee a pivotal aspect of the industry's customer management capabilities. Managing a Customer Advisory Board (CAB) comprising these giants, you've established a rule: if at least five customers commit resources (access to end users, feedback, testing, and data), the product team will explore their requested features in a co-innovation working group.

Situation

During a routine CAB session, the group unanimously identified the addition of an MS Excel download function as a critical enhancement. This feature, they believed, was essential for enhancing user adoption and extracting maximum value from the software. However, as a product leader committed to the core values of integrated planning and based on your strategic foresight, you recognized the potential pitfalls of introducing such a feature.

Response and Leadership

Despite the strong push from the CAB, you decided to reject the request for the MS Excel download function. Initially, this decision met with irritation and surprise, challenging your established rule and the CAB overall. However, steadfast in your role as the driver of product strategy, you convened a session to delve deeper into the underlying issues prompting this request.

You explained to the CAB that while the Excel download feature might seem beneficial superficially, it would ultimately undercut the fundamental benefits of integrated planning—the very feature that differentiated your product and provided significant value to your customers and users. You articulated a vision where dependency on Excel could lead back to fragmented processes, forecasting that the next request would likely be for an Excel upload capability, further diluting the product's core value.

Resolution and Co-Innovation

To address the CAB's concerns constructively, you proposed an alternative approach: focusing on identifying and resolving usability issues that hindered the user experience. This initiative aimed to enhance the existing functionalities without compromising the product's integrated planning capabilities.

You engaged the CAB members in a series of targeted workshops to pinpoint these usability problems. Through these collaborative sessions, you not only gained valuable insights but also redirected the group's energy towards enhancing the core system, thereby reinforcing the value of integrated solutions.

As you face similar situations, you can address them with the following steps:

- **Clear Communication:** Explained your decision in detail to the CAB, emphasizing how the requested feature could compromise the capabilities and value proposition that the customers value.
- **Identifying True Needs**: Instead of dismissing the customer's underlying concerns, your team should engage with them to understand the actual pain points they are experiencing with the current solution.
- **Commitment to Action**: Initiate a co-innovation workstream focused on enhancing the raised product concerns. This approach ensured that improvements are aligned with genuine user needs without compromising the product's strategic vision.

Outcome

This strategic pivot not only alleviated the initial shock and dissatisfaction among the CAB members but also transformed them into active proponents of the software. Many members became eager to share their positive experiences, contributing to case studies and testimonials that underscored the benefits of staying true to integrated planning principles.

Your engagement strategy emphasized the importance of direct participation and feedback, which played a crucial role in aligning the product development with genuine customer needs. By involving CAB members in problem-solving and beta testing of new solutions, you fostered a sense of ownership and advocacy among the users.

Lessons Learned

1. **Leadership in Product Management**: The ability to say "no" is at least as crucial as saying "yes." Effective product leaders guide their products not just by market demands but by a vision that ensures long-term value.
2. **Customer-Centric Innovation**: Engaging customers in identifying real problems rather than superficial solutions ensures that product enhancements are genuinely valuable and not just momentarily appeasing.
3. **Building Advocacy**: Transforming customer feedback into actionable insight creates advocates who believe in the product's direction and are willing to publicly support it.

This case study exemplifies how a product leader can maintain control over the product's strategic direction, even in the face of strong customer opinions, turning potential conflicts into opportunities for deeper engagement and product advocacy.

A clear "No" to a feature request, when backed by a strong rationale and a commitment to addressing the underlying needs, can enhance credibility and leadership in the eyes of customers. This approach not only supports sustained product success but also fosters a deeper, more collaborative relationship with key users.

B2B vs. B2C Environment Considerations

As with engagement strategies in general, the specific tactics you use within each of these pillars may differ depending on whether you serve B2B or B2C customers.

B2B Environment: Focus on building relationships with key decision-makers, personalize content and interactions based on specific industry needs, and leverage case studies and testimonials as powerful advocacy tools. Prioritize industry events with targeted audiences, personalize meet-ups around specific pain points, and leverage Customer Advisory Boards for strategic guidance and thought leadership.

B2C Environment: Tap into the power of social media and user-generated content, prioritize gamification and interactive experiences, and build a strong emotional connection with your brand.

The Power of Choice: Building Your Engagement Mix

The beauty of this spectrum is that you can tailor your engagement approach to your specific customer base and budget. Start by identifying your customer segments and their needs. Then, experiment with different types of engagement across the spectrum, measuring the impact on key metrics like customer satisfaction, retention, and advocacy.

Remember, there's no one-size-fits-all approach. The key is to create a dynamic and engaging journey that fosters genuine connections with your customers, ultimately leading them to become your most vocal advocates.

Summary and Key Takeaways

This chapter lays the groundwork for understanding the nuances of different engagement types. As we proceed, we'll explore how to integrate these strategies into a cohesive plan that not only engages customers but actively converts them into advocates, fueling business growth and innovation.

- ✓ **Diverse Engagement Strategies:** Customer engagement encompasses a spectrum of interactions, each playing a role in the path to advocacy. Tailoring engagement strategies to fit different customer needs and contexts is crucial for fostering strong relationships and advocacy.
- ✓ **Balancing Benefits and Challenges:** Each engagement type offers unique benefits but also comes with its own set of challenges, costs and workload. Effective management and execution are key to maximizing benefits and return of investment. Tailoring your

engagement strategy to B2B or B2C audiences is crucial for maximizing impact.
- ✓ **Driving Advocacy:** Engaging customers on multiple levels and through various platforms increases the likelihood of transforming them into advocates. Experiment and measure the effect of different engagement tactics to find the optimal mix for your business. Advocacy is based on trust; trust is earned by delivering on your promises.

Time for Action: Empowering Product Managers with an Integrated Engagement Blueprint

As we conclude this chapter on the diverse spectrum of customer engagement, it's time to pivot from theory to practice. For product managers and product leads, the insights gathered from various engagement strategies serve as a guide to crafting a robust advocacy program. Recognizing the central role that Customer Advisory Boards (CABs) play in this ecosystem, it's imperative to leverage these insights to orchestrate a comprehensive approach tailored to the unique needs and contexts of your customers.

The Role of the Product Manager

Product managers are the orchestrators of customer engagement, positioned uniquely to translate customer interactions into actionable product insights and enhancements. Your role goes beyond managing products; it extends to managing customer relationships. The insights provided in this chapter empower you with the knowledge to engage customers effectively across various platforms and interactions.

Importance of a Coordinated Team Effort

While the product manager leads the charge, successful customer engagement and advocacy require a coordinated team effort. It's crucial to involve cross-functional teams—including marketing, sales, customer service, team admins, and technical support—to ensure a seamless and consistent customer experience. Each team member plays a critical role, contributing different perspectives and expertise to enhance the engagement strategies.

Practical Application: Not Boiling the Ocean

The key to successful customer engagement is not to attempt everything at once—what's often referred to as "boiling the ocean." Instead, focus on strategic initiatives that offer the most significant impact. Evaluate your company's specific needs, customer expectations, and the competitive landscape to prioritize efforts that will deliver the biggest "bang for the buck."

Given the pivotal role CABs play in shaping product direction and enhancing customer engagement, they should be central to your advocacy efforts. CABs offer a unique platform for gathering in-depth insights, testing new ideas, and fostering strong customer relationships. They act as a microcosm of your market, providing feedback and ideas that can drive innovation and product improvements.

Moving forward, the remainder of this book will focus on a pragmatic approach to initiating and maintaining a dynamic customer advocacy pyramid. This integrated approach combines the pillars discussed—personalization, content, community, events, and co-creation—into a cohesive strategy.

As product leads and managers, your goal is to harness the power of customer engagement to turn passive users and customers into active advocates. By understanding the nuances of different engagement types and integrating them into a strategic advocacy plan, you can drive business growth and innovation. Remember, the journey toward customer advocacy is continuous, and it thrives on a foundation of trust and sustained engagement. Let's embark on this journey with a clear vision and a commitment to delivering exceptional value to our customers.

For the remainder of the book, I'll focus on a pragmatic approach to kickstart and spin the flywheel – a comprehensive framework called the Customer Advocacy Pyramid.

3 The Customer Advocacy Pyramid — A Comprehensive Framework for Success

Introduction

In today's rapidly evolving market landscape, fostering deep, meaningful connections with customers is more crucial than ever. This chapter introduces a groundbreaking concept—the Customer Advocacy Pyramid. This pragmatic framework is designed to be a flywheel kickstarter for your customer engagement efforts, integrating various dimensions of interaction into a cohesive strategy that amplifies advocacy and drives sustainable growth.

The Customer Advocacy Pyramid encapsulates the full spectrum of customer engagement, blending personalized interactions with strategic content-driven initiatives and vibrant community engagement. It is a comprehensive model that organizes Executive Advisory Boards, Customer Advisory Boards, Co-Innovation Workstreams, User Conferences, Company Events, Summits, Customer References & Testimonials, and both internal and external user groups into a structured, scalable system.

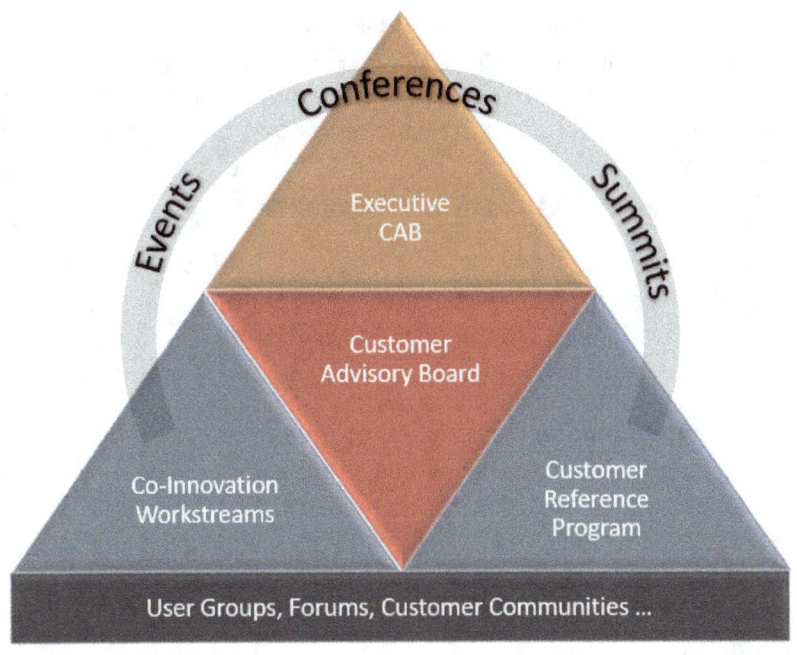

Figure 3: The Customer Advocacy Pyramid

Components of the Customer Advocacy Pyramid

1. Customer Advisory Boards (CABs): Positioned at the center of the pyramid, CABs are critical for gathering actionable insights and fostering deep relationships with key customers. CABs vary in structure to cater to different strategic needs:

- **Executive Advisory Boards:** Focus on high-level, executive-to-executive relationships.

- **(Product-centric) Customer Advisory Boards:** Involve business and IT users, addressing operational and tactical aspects of product use and development.

Whether executive-focused or product-focused, these boards are instrumental in shaping product strategy and ensuring alignment with market needs.

2. Co-Innovation Workstreams: These are collaborative projects involving customers and company teams to develop new solutions or enhance existing products, driven by direct customer input and co-creation efforts. These co-innovation projects are initiated out of CABs and the progress and outcomes are reported back to the CABs and can be showcased at Executive Advisory Boards, Events, or Conferences.

3. User Conferences, Summits, and Company Events: These gatherings are excellent opportunities for networking, education, and showcasing product innovations. They provide a platform for discussions and networking, often yielding valuable testimonials and case studies.

4. User Groups, Communities, and Meet-Ups: User groups, communities, and meet-ups form a vital tier within the Customer Advocacy Pyramid, offering platforms for users to connect, share, and grow together around your product or service. This engagement layer leverages both online and offline formats to foster a sense of belonging among users, providing a space for them to exchange insights and discuss challenges and benefits of your products.

5. Customer Reference Program: Customer references and testimonials are crucial for building credibility and demonstrating the real-world value of products. Customer success stories can be leveraged across various platforms to enhance the company's market position. In chapter 6, we will dive deep into6 Amplifying Product Success Through Customer References and Testimonials.

The Customer Advocacy Pyramid is not just a theoretical model; it is a practical, actionable framework that integrates all key aspects of customer engagement. By centering your strategy around CABs and supporting it with a spectrum of engagement activities, you can build a robust advocacy program that not only meets but exceeds your strategic objectives. In subsequent chapters, we will delve deeper into each component of the pyramid, providing you with detailed guidance on how to implement and optimize these strategies effectively.

Customer Advisory Boards are the foundation of customer engagement and the center of the Customer Advocacy Pyramid. Well-executed CABs can serve as a strategic asset in distinguishing your company from the competition. Implementing these boards effectively requires adherence to several key guidelines designed to maximize benefits for both your organization and your customers. It is important to recognize that these benefits come with necessary commitments of time and budget. However, from my experience, the investment in any of the two types of customer advisory boards—executive or product focused—is profoundly worthwhile.

Benefit of CABs

CABs are an excellent and powerful way of building customer engagement and advocacy. Let's have a look at the benefits of engaging customers via Customer Advisory Boards:

Customer Benefits

- Get early insights into your product strategy and planning.
- Increase access and engagement with product team.
- Peer-to-peer knowledge sharing and networking with peers.
- Influence product development during the full development cycle.
- Get to know and build personal relationships with the product team.
- Securely exchange information in a clear legal framework

Product Organization Benefits

- Deepen customer relationships.
- Verify product strategy and positioning.
- Clarify requirements and constraints.
- Validate importance of product requirements.
- Increase revenue and product adoption.
- Build trust and community.
- Get to know and build personal relationships with the customers (i.e. real people).
- Securely exchange information in a clear legal framework.

Establish a formal CAB empowered to shape your future.

- **Approach**: Carefully select members, structure meetings with clear agendas, and use collaborative digital tools for ongoing exchange between sessions.
- **Benefits**: Gain invaluable product insights, prioritize your product decisions with a market view, and turn advocates into partners by giving them a voice.
- **Challenges**: Requires meticulous planning and active management, ensuring both face-to-face and digital interactions feel meaningful to CAB members.

Key Characteristics of Effective CABs

- **Mutually Beneficial:** CABs drive objectives that benefit both your product and the customers involved, enhancing the overall value of your products.

- **Strategic Communication:** They facilitate regular interactions between council members and your product team, fostering a cycle of feedback and influence that shapes strategy, market approaches, roadmaps, and product development.

- **Expert Leadership:** Comprised of senior executives and visionary leaders, CABs thrive on rich, two-way discussions that cover strategic topics relevant to both parties.

- **Resource Commitment:** Both sides commit resources to ensure productive collaboration and outcome-oriented discussions.

Executive and Customer Advisory Boards – A Comparison

	Executive Advisory Board	Customer Advisory Board
Host / Sponsor	Founder / Board / CPO / Head of Product	CPO / Head of Product / Product Manager
Target customer audience	Execs from strategic customers, segment agnostic, key influencers	B2B: Business and IT representatives from existing customers B2C: strategic influencers, Power Users
Customer member traits	C-Level, decision makers, thought leaders	Corporate influence, impact, and authority Representative of future/vision for market segments, geographies, industries, etc.
Membership	Invitation only by sponsor > 10 active members	Invitation only by sponsor > 10 active members max 30 members
Customer Feedback	Interaction, feedback, and guidance on company and product strategy; domain trends and customer priorities	Interaction, feedback, and guidance on geographic / industry / line of business strategy; strategic dialogue and feedback on future product innovation

Meeting frequency	1-2 times annually, rotated by geography for customer proximity	In-person 1-2 times annually, rotated by geography for customer proximity, supplemented by 4-6 virtual meetings
Meeting duration	1-2 days	2-3 days (one day usually dedicated to focus topics / deep dives for selected participants)
Meeting agenda	Standing agenda including trends, strategy, roadmaps	Mixture of customer-led and own-led, proven practices sharing, mixture of standing and customer-driven agenda

The Role of Product Management

At the heart of the Customer Advocacy Pyramid is the product leader—the orchestrator of customer engagement. As a product lead, your role extends beyond the traditional boundaries of product development; you are also the prime mover in driving customer advocacy. In this dynamic, it's crucial not to stretch too thin ("don't boil the ocean") but rather focus on impactful activities that offer the "biggest bang for the buck."

This approach means strategically deploying resources where they can generate the most substantial impact, relying on a well-coordinated team to execute various initiatives effectively.

Recruiting CAB Customer Candidates

- **Identifying Candidates**: Target strategic customers who represent your ideal market segments and have a vested interest in the product's success.

- **Invitation Process**: Personalize invitations to clearly outline the benefits and expectations of joining the CAB.

- **Inclusivity**: Strive for diversity across industry segments, company sizes, and geographical regions to ensure well-rounded insights.

- **Commitment**: Emphasize the importance of consistent participation and active contribution to maximize the value for all parties.

Structuring the CAB Planning and Execution Team

Recognizing the significant demands on a product leads' time, it is vital to establish a dedicated team to manage the intricacies of the Customer Advocacy Pyramid. While the product lead acts as the sponsor and strategic leader, the day-to-day operations should be handled by team members specializing in different areas of customer engagement. This structure allows the product manager to maintain oversight without being bogged down by the operational details of every activity.

To effectively manage and harness the potential of the Customer Advocacy Pyramid, it's crucial to structure a team with clearly defined roles and responsibilities. These roles are designed to cover the various facets of customer engagement ensuring that each component of the pyramid is optimally supported. It's important to note that depending on the size and resources of the organization, one person may need to assume multiple roles, particularly in smaller teams or startups.

Key Roles for Effective CABs and the Customer Advocacy Pyramid

1. **Customer Advocacy Lead**

    - **Responsibilities**: Serves as the strategic visionary and chief advocate for the customer within the organization. Sets the overarching goals for customer engagement and advocacy, ensuring alignment with broader business objectives. Guides the strategic direction of the Customer Advisory Boards and other pyramid components.

    - **Skills Needed**: Strong leadership, strategic thinking, and excellent communication skills to articulate vision and align various teams.

2. **Customer Engagement Admin**

    - **Responsibilities**: Directly manages the operational aspects of the Customer Advisory Boards, user groups, and community meet-ups. Facilitates meetings, drafts agendas, ensures follow-up on action items, and maintains ongoing communication with CAB members.
    - **Skills Needed**: Excellent organizational and project management skills, adept at relationship building and maintaining engagement over time.

3. **Community Coordinator**

    - **Responsibilities**: Oversees online and offline communities and user groups. Engages members, stimulates discussions, manages content, and moderates to ensure a positive and productive environment.
    - **Skills Needed**: Strong interpersonal skills, community management experience, and a knack for creating engaging content that resonates with the community.

4. **Event Planner**

    - **Responsibilities**: Coordinates all logistics for user conferences, workshops, and other events that are part of the advocacy program. Works with vendors, secures venues, and manages attendee lists.
    - **Skills Needed**: Strong logistical planning skills, attention to detail, and ability to manage multiple tasks simultaneously under tight deadlines.

5. **Data Analyst**

    - **Responsibilities**: Tracks and analyzes data from various customer engagement activities to measure impact and effectiveness. Provides insights that help refine strategies and tactics within the Customer Advocacy Pyramid.
    - **Skills Needed**: Strong analytical skills, proficiency in data analysis tools, and the ability to derive meaningful insights from complex datasets.

The Flywheel in Action

In product management, understanding how to orchestrate various customer engagement strategies into a coherent and effective model is crucial. The Customer Advocacy Pyramid connects all components of customer engagement—from Customer Advisory Boards (CABs) and Executive Advisory Boards to co-innovation workstreams, and impactful customer events. Let's explore how these elements integrate to drive continuous improvement and growth, propelling your products and company forward.

The concept of a flywheel in business is powerful; it represents a self-reinforcing cycle that gains momentum with each customer interaction. In the context of the Customer Advocacy Pyramid, each component—whether it's a CAB, user group, or a customer testimonial—adds energy to the flywheel, enhancing the overall effectiveness of customer advocacy.

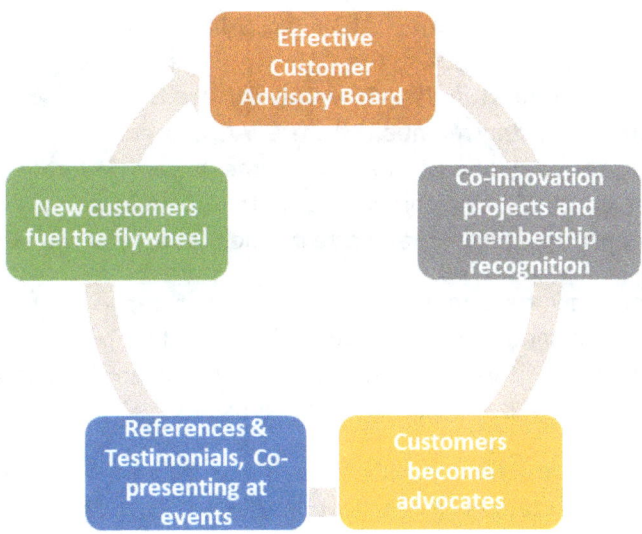

Figure 4: The Engagement-Advocacy Flywheel in Action

Success Story: Harnessing Customer Engagement at SAP

Introduction

During my tenure as a product lead at SAP for the Trade Management suite, I had the unique opportunity to witness and direct the transformative power of strategic customer engagement. The story of SAP's customer engagement and advocacy flywheel is a vivid illustration of how integrated customer engagement can propel a product and a company to new heights.

Building the Foundation with CPAC

The journey began with the establishment of the Consumer Products Advisory Council (CPAC), an EAB composed of leading names in the consumer products industry such as PepsiCo, The Coca Cola Company, and Red Bull. This council set a strategic direction, identifying broad industry needs and opportunities which informed the more focused agendas of our Customer Advisory Boards (CABs). CPAC was not just an executive forum for networking and discussion; it was the springboard of our customer engagement strategy.

Expanding the Engagement: CABs and Co-Innovation

Transitioning from the EAB to the CAB, we delved deeper into customer challenges and opportunities. The CAB for Trade Management, which started with recruiting members from CPAC and gradually expanded to include a wider array of customers over time, became a fertile ground for identifying specific pain points and potential innovations that could directly impact the efficiency and effectiveness of their businesses.

The diverse membership facilitated a broader range of perspectives, enriching the co-innovation process. It allowed us to tap into the collective insights of some of the most innovative companies in the sector, guiding the development of our Trade Management suite.

Our approach to co-innovation was particularly meticulous. Past experiences have taught us that unchecked customer-driven requests by single, powerful customers could lead to product features that, while initially demanded, ultimately went unused. To avoid this, we instituted a rule: at least five CAB members needed to commit to actively co-innovate and utilize new features. This policy ensured that our innovations were market-driven and widely applicable, not just tailored to the whims of the large and powerful ones.

The Flywheel in Action

The real magic happened when these components—the CAB and co-innovation initiatives—began to interact seamlessly, creating a self-reinforcing cycle of engagement and improvement.

Within the CAB, co-innovation workstreams were established as a method to harness real user feedback and actual customer data, vital for developing solutions that not only resonated with our customers but also provided tangible improvements to their business processes. This approach was rooted in a pragmatic rule: any feature or improvement required the active commitment of at least five CAB members, ensuring that the developments were genuinely desired and would be utilized, avoiding the pitfalls of unused features.

Key to maintaining the momentum of the flywheel was our vibrant customer community. We met twice a year in person and six times virtually, creating regular touchpoints that kept the dialogue open and the ideas flowing. Remarkably, despite the competitive nature of some of the member companies, such as Red Bull, PepsiCo and The Coca Cola Company, these firms hosted CAB meetings in their offices. This gesture underscored the collaborative spirit and mutual benefit of the CAB, transcending competitive barriers in favor of shared product advancement.

These meetings were not just about discussion—they were about action and results. The co-innovation workstreams identified during these gatherings led to multiple successful innovations, each enhancing our product suite's capabilities and directly addressing the nuanced needs of our customers.

Showcasing Success: SAPPHIRE and Beyond

SAP's annual flagship conference, SAPPHIRE, became a prime stage to showcase the fruits of this robust customer engagement. Members from our CAB shared their success stories, discussing how collaborative efforts and customer-centric innovations have significantly enhanced their success. These testimonials were not just stories; they were powerful validations of our product's impact, echoed in the discussions held with industry analysts and covered by the press at SAPPHIRE. This exposure was invaluable and led to notable improvements in our market ratings.

Moreover, the conference allowed us to leverage existing infrastructure for creating high-quality video testimonials and conducting in-depth customer interviews. These assets became crucial elements of our marketing strategy, amplifying the voice of our customers and providing authentic proof of our product's value.

A Model of Integrated Strategy

At SAP, the dynamic interplay between various components of the Customer Advocacy Pyramid—Executive Advisory Boards (EAB), Customer Advisory Boards (CAB), co-innovation workstreams, and vibrant customer communities—formed a powerful flywheel that drove continuous product enhancement and customer engagement. This synergy was not accidental but the result of strategic planning and active management, particularly within the Trade Management suite.

The integration of EAB insights, CAB initiatives, co-innovation workstreams, and a robust customer community exemplifies the flywheel effect in action. Each component fed into the next, continuously improving the product while increasing customer satisfaction and advocacy. This cycle of engagement, innovation, and advocacy not only propelled the Trade Management suite forward but also cemented SAP's reputation as a customer-centric organization.

This story of SAP's Trade Management is more than a narrative of successful product management—it is a blueprint for how integrated customer engagement can transform a business, turning satisfied customers into active advocates and driving sustainable growth in a competitive marketplace.

This model demonstrates that true customer advocacy stems from deep engagement and a commitment to mutual success. It shows that when companies listen to and genuinely collaborate with their customers, they do not just sell products—they build enduring partnerships and create a formidable market presence.

The Role of Product

As a product lead, your task is to steer this flywheel, maintaining its momentum and ensuring each component works harmoniously with the others. You're not just managing a product; you're fostering an ecosystem of engaged customers whose feedback and advocacy become integral to your product's success. Here's how to manage this effectively:

- **Lead, Don't Do Everything**: Establish a team where members are empowered with specific roles within the Customer Advocacy Pyramid. Your role is to provide direction and support, ensuring that the strategic vision is clear and that operational tasks are effectively executed.
- **Use Data to Drive Decisions**: Regularly review the impact of each component of the pyramid on overall customer satisfaction and product improvements. Use this data to fine-tune your approach and focus resources where they are most effective.

B2B vs. B2C Environment Considerations

The dynamics of the Customer Advocacy Pyramid can vary significantly between B2B and B2C contexts:

- **B2B Environments**: Here, the focus is on depth. Building long-term relationships and establishing thought leadership through detailed case studies and in-depth user engagement can have a profound impact on customer retention and acquisition.
- **B2C Environments**: Volume and virality are key. Encouraging social sharing and leveraging user-generated content can rapidly enhance product visibility and adoption.

Connecting It All Together

The Customer Advocacy Pyramid is not just a framework but a strategic approach that integrates various facets of customer engagement to drive product success. By understanding how to effectively connect CABs, co-innovation efforts, events, and community engagement, product managers can create a self-sustaining cycle of advocacy that boosts customer satisfaction and drives growth.

- **Integrated Strategy:** The Customer Advocacy Pyramid aligns all customer engagement activities under a cohesive strategy, maximizing their collective impact.
- **Product Lead's Role**: As the orchestrator of the pyramid, the product lead ensures that each component contributes effectively to the overall strategy.

- **Adaptability**: Tailor the approach to fit the unique needs of your B2B or B2C context, focusing on the aspects that will most significantly drive engagement and advocacy in your market.

Engaging customers effectively is an art that hinges on a straightforward yet powerful formula: providing value and cultivating commitment. Here's how to apply this formula to create meaningful connections with your customers:

1. **Provide Value Through Early Insights and Know-How Sharing**: Offer your customers something that goes beyond the product itself. This could be in the form of early access to new features, exclusive insights into industry trends, or valuable knowledge sharing that helps them achieve their business goals. By doing so, you position your product and company as a trusted partner rather than just a vendor.

2. **Encourage Active Participation**: The more time customers invest in your product, the deeper their commitment tends to grow. As part of co-innovation workstreams, invite them to participate in beta tests, feedback sessions, or product development workshops. Their involvement not only makes your product better but also deepens their loyalty as they see their suggestions being taken seriously and implemented.

The Customer Advocacy Pyramid components provide a platform for customers to connect not only with your organization but also with each other. This network builds a robust ecosystem around your product, where customers feel they belong to a group of like-minded individuals with shared interests and challenges.

As members of the exclusive community, they engage and share their experiences, they develop a collective identity that is aligned with your organization's values and goals. This sense of shared identity helps to cement their loyalty to your product and increases their likelihood of advocating for you within their own networks.

By integrating these strategies into your customer engagement efforts, you create a powerful synergy that enhances customer satisfaction, loyalty, and ultimately, advocacy. This approach not only supports sustainable business growth but also builds a loyal base of customers who are excited to grow along with your product.

In the following chapter, we will delve into the practical steps for implementing the key component of the Customer Advocacy Pyramid, providing you with a detailed CAB "cookbook" that outlines actionable strategies and tips for success.

4 The Customer Advisory Board Cookbook

Introduction

In the previous chapter, we discovered that Customer Advisory Boards (CABs) are exclusive, invitation-only groups comprising strategic customers who are integral to advancing your product vision and strategy to reach and keep product market fit.

Imagine a room buzzing with passionate voices. Product leaders like yourself are shoulder-to-shoulder with your most dedicated customers, exchanging ideas and brainstorming solutions. This isn't a fantasy – it's the magic of a Customer Advisory Board (CAB).

In the world of product management, where innovation reigns supreme, a CAB can be your secret weapon. This chapter will unveil the power of CABs, transforming them from a vague term to a cornerstone of your product success strategy. We'll explore real-world examples, practical tips, and best practices to leverage your CAB for groundbreaking results. No surprise, CABs serve as a foundational element of customer engagement and are at the center piece of the customer advocacy pyramid.

CABs are distinct in their composition—not just made up of your largest or most vocal customers, but rather those deeply committed to your product's success and its future trajectory. Members are carefully selected for their strategic importance and ability to contribute meaningfully to the product dialogue.

When setting up a CAB, it's essential to clearly define its mission and engage members who are actual customers and users of your product, excluding prospects and sales personnel to maintain the council's focus and integrity. This approach ensures that the CAB remains an effective and trusted advisory body, focused solely on fostering product excellence and strategic, future-looking innovation.

In this chapter, we will delve into everything you need to know about Customer Advisory Boards, from their evaluation to leveraging their outcomes, step by step.

Professionally managed CABs are built on several critical success factors:

- **Company Participation**: Ensure a minimum of 10 companies are involved in executive or customer advisory boards, but limit

participation to no more than 30 to maintain an intimate, manageable community. The CAB needs to be aligned with your product strategy and future aspirations to be effective.
- **Shared Leadership**: Appoint a customer co-lead to share leadership responsibilities, enhancing the council's collaborative nature. The co-leadership can change year over year.
- **Clear Commitments**: Define the roles and responsibilities of the council host/sponsor clearly, and ensure all participants are aware of the engagement level required.
- **Meeting Frequency and Planning**: Set a recurring meeting schedule and send out invites well in advance—sometimes up to a year—to ensure high attendance.
- **Maintain a Non-Sales Focus**: Focus on providing a platform for influence rather than sales to respect the advisory intent of the council.
- **Prompt Follow-Up**: Address action items and respond to council queries promptly to maintain momentum and show respect for members' contributions.

Step-by-Step Guide for Effective Customer Advisory Boards

This chapter offers a detailed, step-by-step guide to establishing and managing a successful Customer Advisory Board (CAB). By following this comprehensive "recipe," you will ensure that your CAB not only meets but surpasses its goals, delivering substantial value to your product, organization, and career.

Importantly, this guide is applicable to both Executive Advisory Boards and Product-centric CABs. While there are distinctions between these two types of boards—as discussed in the previous chapter—the fundamental setup and management process remain consistent across both.

Whether you're focusing on executive-level industry trends or product-specific feedback, the principles outlined in this chapter will help you create a CAB that is both effective and aligned with your strategic objectives. By adhering to this proven framework, you'll engage your most important customers and harness their insights to propel your product forward in the market.

To ensure your CAB is effective, it's essential to carefully plan and execute each phase of its lifecycle. Below, we outline the key steps involved in setting up and operating a CAB. This "CAB Cookbook" will equip you with the tools and strategies needed to harness the full potential of your customer advisory efforts.

The step-by-step guide comprises the following 5 steps:

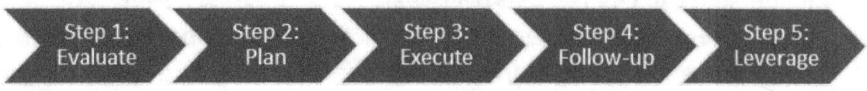

Figure 5: 5-Step Customer Advisory Board Recipe

By following these structured steps, organizations can maximize the impact of their Customer Advisory Boards, turning strategic customer insights into actionable outcomes that drive growth and innovation.

Step 1: Evaluate the Need for Customer Advisory Boards

To assess whether your organization should establish one or more CABs, or possibly determine that none is needed, employ this straightforward and actionable evaluation process. By systematically addressing these questions, you can build a strong case for the formation of a CAB that aligns closely with your organization's strategic priorities and operational needs. This thorough evaluation will not only support internal approval processes but also ensure that the CAB is purposefully integrated into your broader business strategy.

a. **Identify your Organizational Needs**

While the advantages of CABs may seem self-evident due to their proven effectiveness and the strong endorsement they receive, it's essential to carefully articulate and document the rationale behind initiating such a board. This foundational step is not just about justifying the need; it also involves detailing the specific requirements for setting up successful CABs. Here are several evaluation prompts designed to help pinpoint the necessity for CABs within your organization. Additionally, these insights will prove invaluable when justifying the time and financial commitments to your management.

- **Question:** Does your organization need or would benefit from feedback on new capabilities, innovations, or strategic directions?

- **Action:** Review your product strategy and strategic goals to identify areas where customer input could be crucial.

Well-managed Customer Advisory Councils or other customer engagements deliver great ROI (Jensen, 2017)

- More business from customer advisory boards than from non-members
- Higher customer loyalty
- Strategic direction from trusted customer contacts
- Acceleration in referrals and testimonials process

b. Assess Customer Interest and Relationships

- **Question:** Do you have a sufficient number of interested customers to initiate a CAB? Are the interested customers representative of your target market (segments)?

- **Action:** Compile a list of potential members who have shown interest in deeper engagement. Engage with Account teams and customer success teams early. Manage the customer expectations as CABs are exclusive and by invitation only.

- **Question:** Are there long-term customer relationships that could benefit from more formalized engagement?

- **Action:** Identify key accounts that have been integral to your business and would provide valuable, continuous feedback.

c. Identify Customer Needs

- **Question:** Are there ongoing customer requests, concerns, or specific needs for closer alignment with the product organization?

- **Action:** Gather feedback through surveys, direct communications, or recent interactions (customer success, support, etc.) to pinpoint areas where a CAB could provide valuable insights.

- **Question:** Is there an existing flow of communication with customers that suggests the need for more structured discussions?
- **Action:** Analyze the frequency and quality of current interactions to determine if a CAB could enhance these exchanges.

d. **Capacity for Follow-Up**

- **Question:** Does your organization have the capacity to act on the insights and maintain the momentum post-CAB meetings?
- **Action:** Ensure that you have the necessary staff and resources to implement feedback and manage ongoing CAB activities effectively. That's especially critical for PM leads and product managers pushing for CABs. Without proper administrative support, planning and executing effective CABs are at high risk.

e. **Market Awareness and Influence**

- **Question:** Is there a need to enhance market awareness or identify industry influencers through a CAB?
- **Action:** Consider whether a CAB could help in promoting your products and gathering pivotal market intelligence.

f. **Budget and Resources**

- **Question:** Are there available resources and budget to support the establishment and maintenance of a CAB? Especially, as a product lead, do you have administrative support?
- **Action:** Allocate budget and designate team members to manage CAB operations, ensuring alignment with financial planning and your team capacity.

g. **Positioning of the CAB**

- **Question:** What will be the focus of the CAB — specific market segments, product lines, products, product modules, or a combination of topics?

- **Action:** Define the scope based on strategic business areas where customer input would be most beneficial, deciding between specialized or comprehensive advisory boards.

By following these steps, you can effectively assess the need for one ore multiple CABs and set the foundation for a successful advisory board that aligns with your strategic business needs.

Step 2: Plan Customer Advisory Boards

Once the decision to establish a CAB has been made, planning and managing these boards become substantial projects in their own right. This chapter will guide you through the essential steps for planning successful advisory councils, as depicted in Figure 4, and provide insights on iterating these steps effectively after each CAB session.

Organizing a CAB requires meticulous planning and coordination. We will cover all essential aspects to help ensure a successful CAB event from preliminary arrangements to post-event follow-ups. We will cover the following topics in the planning phase:

- **Initial Set-Up, Team Engagement, and Logistics**
- **CAB Project Plan including Scheduling and Financial Planning**
- **Customer Advisory Council Communications Approach**

Let's start with investigating the initial set-up of CABs, staffing the project team and some logistical considerations.

Step 2a: Initial Setup and Team Engagement
Define Team Roles and Confirm the Project Team

Share a CAB Charter document that explains the CABs importance, objectives, team set-up, and project plan.

- **Product Manager**: Oversees product-related discussions and integrates feedback into the product roadmap.
- **Facilitator**: Manages the flow of the meeting, ensuring all voices are heard and the agenda is adhered to.
- **Project Coordinator**: Handles logistical and administrative tasks.
- **Executive Sponsor**: Provides leadership support and ensures alignment with strategic goals.

Choosing the Right Location

- **Target Audience Consideration**: Choose a location that is accessible and appealing to the global or local target audience as needed.
- **Market Focus**: Decide on hosting in growth markets versus established markets based on strategic priorities.
- **Venue Selection**:
    - **Internal Location**: Selecting a company facility can save costs and give participants insight into the company culture.
    - **External Location**: Choosing an external, representative venue can provide a neutral, comfortable setting conducive to open discussion and networking.

Logistical Arrangements

- **Venue Booking**: Secure a venue that supports the technical and comfort needs of the event.
- **Travel Arrangements**: Plan and possibly sponsor travel for attendees, particularly if they are coming from out of town.
- **Catering Services**: Arrange meals and refreshments that cater to the preferences and dietary restrictions of the attendees.
- **Technology Setup**: Ensure availability of necessary tech support for presentations, remote participation (if applicable), and real-time collaboration tools.

Step 2b: CAB Project Plan including Scheduling and Financial Planning

A well-structured Customer Advisory Board (CAB) project plan is crucial to ensure the seamless execution of your meetings and maximize their strategic impact. By meticulously scheduling activities and aligning financial resources, you set the groundwork for a productive and engaging event. Meanwhile, thoughtful financial planning guarantees a memorable experience, balancing the costs of venue, catering, and logistics while providing a valuable environment where ideas can flourish.

Ultimately, an organized project plan not only streamlines the CAB process but also reinforces the value of the board, ensuring it meets strategic objectives and delivers a strong return on investment.

Create a Project Plan:

Outline all tasks, assign responsibilities, and set deadlines. You can find a well-structured CAB project plan template in chapter Customer Advisory Board (CAB) Project Plan below or you can download this template and many more interesting holistic product management materials at www.productand.com/HolisticProductManagementToolKit.

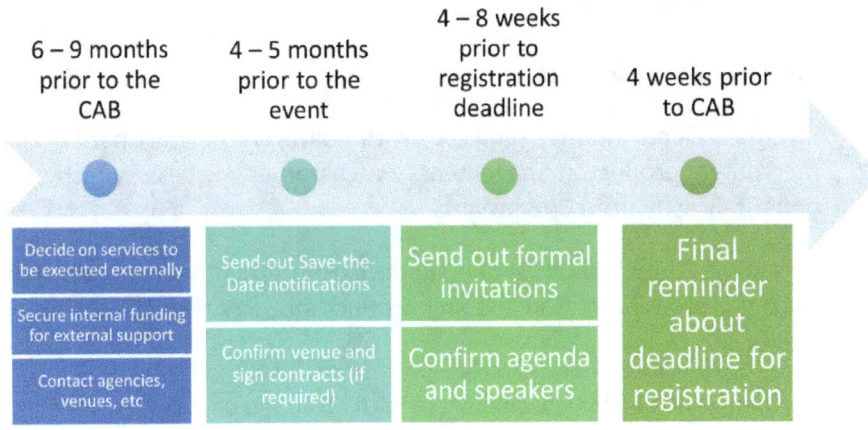

Figure 6: High-level CAB Timeline

CAB Timing Considerations:

- Preferably schedule meetings in **Q2 and Q3** to maximize attendance and engagement. Hence, I provided the template project plan for illustrative meeting dates mid-April and mid-September.

- Avoid overlaps with major customer events, own flagship conferences, industry events (e.g. NRF for retail), and competitor events.

- Do not schedule during holiday seasons to ensure higher participation.

- Ensure there is no conflict with the Executive Advisory Board schedule.

- Consider co-locating the CAB with another event if it adds value and convenience.

Determine Sponsoring/Funding:

Securing proper funding for a Customer Advisory Board (CAB) meeting is crucial for delivering a well-organized, valuable event that maximizes customer engagement. Here's a breakdown of how to identify budget sources and allocate funds effectively:

1. **Identify Budget Sources**:

- **Internal Departments**: Engage with different departments like marketing, product management, or customer success, which can benefit directly from CAB insights.

- **Executive Sponsorship**: Obtain support from executive sponsors who have a vested interest in shaping product strategy through customer feedback.

- **Partner Contributions**: Collaborate with strategic partners or agencies who may want to contribute in exchange for branding opportunities or exposure.
  Note: Consider partner contributions with maximum caution. In fact, I would not recommend taking this path as the actual CAB objectives and nature of the events are seriously at risk. Only use that option if there is no other way to properly fund the CAB.

2. **Allocate Funds**:

- **Venue & Logistics**:

    - *Venue Costs*: Choose a location that fits your budget and ensures high attendance. Consider conference rooms at partner offices or reputable hotels.

    - *Logistics*: Account for the cost of transportation between the hotel and venue, A/V equipment, and registration.

- **Travel & Accommodations**:

    - *Travel*: Provide travel support or reimbursements for key customers, if applicable, to reduce barriers to attendance.

    - *Accommodation*: Book comfortable hotel rooms in close proximity to the venue to enhance the attendee experience.

- **Meals & Refreshments**:

    - *Meals*: Allocate for breakfast, lunch, and dinner receptions, ensuring meals cater to varied preferences and dietary restrictions.

    - *Refreshments*: Offer snacks and drinks during breaks to maintain energy levels.

- **Customer Giveaways**:

    - *Promotional Items*: Offer branded giveaways like stationery, USB drives, or apparel to create a positive, lasting impression.

    - *Experience Gifts*: Consider unique items like local artisan goods or sustainable merchandise that reflect your company's values.

    - **Note**: Be mindful of tax exemption limits for customer giveaways to ensure compliance with regional regulations.

- **Other Expenses**:

- *Event Marketing Materials*: Design and print brochures, banners, and event signage to promote your brand and create a professional ambiance.

- *Event Staffing*: Include costs for event coordinators, registration personnel, and A/V technicians as needed.

By thoughtfully determining sponsorship and funding sources and allocating the budget, you can create a seamless, valuable CAB meeting that fosters engagement and leaves customers feeling appreciated and valued.

3. **Update Events Calendar**: Record all planned meeting dates for the CAB in the company's master events calendar.

- **Identify Key Dates**: Establish regular meeting dates (both virtual and in-person) in the calendar. Plan these 6-9 months before the event.

- **Sync with Company Events**: Ensure no conflicts with major company events like conferences or launches. Consider hosting CAB meetings around large industry conferences to optimize travel plans.

- **Notify Members**: Send "Save the Date" invitations at least 4-5 months in advance.

Step 2c: Customer Advisory Council Communications Approach

Finally, we develop a communication strategy that includes pre-event information, ongoing updates, and post-event summaries to engage participants throughout the process.

To ensure that every stage of your CAB is communicated effectively, a robust communication strategy is vital. This strategy will not only prepare participants for CAB membership and the CAB meetings, but also set the stage for active and meaningful engagement.

Here are the key CAB communications to consider, designed to streamline interaction and ensure participants are well-informed and prepared for the CAB meetings. You'll find a few communication templates for the various communication types in chapter Templates: Communication Types and Best Practices or you can download these templates and many more interesting holistic product management materials at www.productand.com/HolisticProductManagementToolKit.

Pre-CAB Communications:

- **CAB Membership Invitation** to formally invite selected customers to become members of the CAB.

    - **Content**: Explain the benefits of joining the CAB, what is expected of members, and the strategic importance of their contributions.

    - **Action**: Request confirmation of their participation and provide a CAB charter to help them understand the scope of the engagement.

- **Invite CAM members to Collaboration Group** to create a platform for ongoing communication.

    - **Content**: Offer details about the collaboration group's objectives, how it will be used for pre- and post-event discussions, and logistical planning.

    - **Action**: Provide a link to join the group and encourage members to introduce themselves and share their expectations for the CAB.

- **Save-the-date Communication** to inform potential attendees about the event well in advance.

    - **Content**: Include the event name, date, location, and a brief note on the importance of their presence.

    - **Action**: Encourage recipients to mark their calendars and await further details.

- **Pre-Event Survey** to gather initial thoughts and expectations from the participants, tailoring the meeting to better suit their needs.

    - **Content**: Ask specific questions related to the agenda topics, logistical preferences, and any particular areas they hope to explore during the CAB.

- **Action**: Use the responses to fine-tune the agenda and focus discussions on the areas of greatest interest to members.

- **CAB Meeting Invitation** to confirm attendance and provide detailed information about the upcoming CAB meeting.

  - **Content**: Include a detailed agenda, logistical details (venue, travel arrangements, accommodations), and any preparatory materials needed for the meeting.

  - **Action**: Ask for RSVPs to finalize attendance and accommodate any special requests (e.g., dietary restrictions).

Following a CAB meeting, it's crucial to maintain momentum and nurture the relationships that have been strengthened during the event. A well-structured post-CAB communication strategy ensures that the insights gained are actioned, participants feel valued, and the engagement continues to build until the next meeting.

Implementing a post-CAB communication strategy will help solidify the connections made during the meeting and enhance the value of the CAB for all participants. It ensures that every member feels acknowledged and sees the tangible outcomes of their involvement, which is essential for fostering long-term commitment and participation in future CAB initiatives.

Each communication should be timely, considerate, and designed to foster a proactive, inclusive community around your product and brand. By keeping these communications regular and relevant, you maintain a vibrant, engaged CAB community ready to support and advocate for your product's success. Here are the key post-CAB communications that should be implemented.

Post-CAB Communications:

- **Thank You Email** to express gratitude to the participants for their contributions and time.

- **Content:** A heartfelt thank you message, a brief recap of the meeting highlights, and an expression of anticipation for future collaborations.
- **Action:** Encourage participants to stay in touch and inform them that more detailed follow-up communications will be forthcoming.

- **Feedback Collection** to gather honest feedback on the meeting to identify successes and areas for improvement.

  - **Content:** Distribute surveys or feedback forms to gather participants' thoughts on the meeting's effectiveness, the relevance of discussed topics, the quality of logistics, and suggestions for future meetings.
  - **Action**: Use a digital platform for easy submission and promise to share a summary of the feedback along with any planned adjustments to address concerns.

- **Action Item Tracking** to keep the momentum going and ensure that agreed- upon action items are executed.

  - **Content**: A detailed list of action items assigned during the CAB, including the responsible parties and the expected timelines.
  - **Action**: Establish a tracking system, possibly within the collaboration group, and schedule regular updates to monitor progress and hold members accountable.

- **Presentation Sharing via Collaboration Group** to provide participants with access to the presentations and materials discussed during the meeting for reference and further reflection.

  - **Content**: Upload all relevant presentations, meeting notes, and additional resources to the established collaboration group.
  - **Action**: Notify participants via email or within the platform once all materials are available and encourage them to review and continue discussions on the platform.

- **Ongoing Engagement** to keep the advisory board members actively engaged and invested in the ongoing development processes and upcoming events.
  - **Content**: Regular updates about the progress made on various projects, upcoming events, or any immediate changes influenced by the CAB discussions.
  - **Action**: Use a mix of newsletters, direct emails, or posts within the collaboration group to maintain a steady stream of communication. Include calls to action where feedback or further input is needed.
- **Post-Event Summary and Next Steps** to encapsulate the key outcomes of the CAB meeting and outline the next steps.
  - **Content**: A two-page summary that includes council highlights, lessons learned, next steps, a link to a shared drive folder containing detailed action items, the agenda, the registration list, and selected customer feedback quotes.
  - **Action**: Distribute this summary to all participants and stakeholders to ensure everyone is aligned on the outcomes and future directions.

All the above communications should be planned with careful consideration of timing, ensuring that each message builds upon the last and contributes to a comprehensive understanding of the upcoming CAB event and the CAB initiative as a whole. Ensure that all communications are clear, concise, and branded consistently to reflect the professionalism of the CAB initiative. The tone should be inviting and inclusive, emphasizing the collaborative nature of the CAB.

By following this structured approach to pre- and post-CAB communications, you can significantly enhance participant engagement and ensure that the CAB meetings are productive and aligned with the strategic goals of both your company and the CAB members.

This proactive communication strategy not only sets the stage for a successful CAB meeting but also fosters a sense of valued partnership among the participants, essential for long-term engagement and mutual success.

For further details on communication templates read chapter Templates: Communication Types and Best Practices or visit www.productand.com/HolisticProductManagementToolKit to access a variety of resources tailored for holistic product management.

Step 3: Execute Customer Advisory Boards

Executing a Customer Advisory Board (CAB) successfully demands thorough planning and an emphasis on engaging and interactive content delivery. Below, we explore the best practices for conducting CAB meetings that not only deliver value to the participants but also create an environment conducive to generating actionable insights.

Plan Agenda and Speakers

Effective CAB meetings hinge on a well-thought-out agenda that balances diverse formats and incorporates input from the members themselves. For further details on agenda best practices and examples read chapter CAB Agenda Template, Best Practices, and Examples or visit www.productand.com/HolisticProductManagementToolKit to access a variety of resources tailored for holistic product management.

1. **Balance the Topics and Formats**:

- Include a mix of interactive sessions, overviews, deep dives, and demonstrations to cater to different learning and engagement styles.
- Plan for dynamic interaction to keep the energy high and the participants engaged.

2. **Involve the Customers**:

- Early in the planning phase, reach out to CAB members to solicit their interests and any specific topics they want to be covered. This ensures the agenda is relevant and adds value to the members.
- Consider rotating hot seats where members can bring up spontaneous topics of discussion.

3. **Innovate the Agenda**:

- Strive to introduce something new in every CAB meeting, whether it's a guest speaker, a new technology demonstration, or a unique collaborative activity, to keep the format fresh and engaging.

Communicate and Confirm Legal Requirements, e.g. Non-Disclosure Agreements (NDAs):

Ensure all participants agree to NDAs if sensitive information is shared during the meeting. This can be managed through digital signature platforms for efficiency.

Prepare Council Feedback Surveys

Develop and share a feedback survey to be completed during or immediately after the meeting. Ensure it's concise yet comprehensive enough to capture insights on the meeting's effectiveness and areas for improvement.

Conduct Pre-Event Briefings for Team Alignment:

Conduct briefings with all stakeholders and staff involved in the CAB to align on the agenda, roles, expectations, and any last-minute changes.

Document Meeting Minutes

Appoint a dedicated scribe to take detailed notes during the meeting, capturing key points, decisions, and action items. These minutes are crucial for post-meeting follow-up and historical reference.

Execution and Follow-Up

- **Onsite Coordination:** Assign staff to handle logistics from registration to assisting participants and managing any onsite issues.

- **Documentation and Communication**: Keep thorough records of discussions and decisions. Post-meeting, share a detailed summary with all participants and stakeholders, outlining key takeaways, action items, and the date of the next meeting.

- **Leverage Technology**: Use collaborative tools to share documents, gather ongoing feedback, and facilitate communication between meetings to maintain engagement.

Building in Time for Socializing and Networking

Recognize the importance of informal interactions:

- Schedule social events like dinners or receptions to encourage informal networking.

- Allow time for breakfast or coffee before the meeting starts to warm up the discussions.

Wrapping Up the Meeting

- **Meeting Recap**: Conclude with a session summarizing the discussions, highlighting actionable items, and setting the stage for the next meeting.

- **Next Steps**: Clearly communicate the next steps, including how the feedback will be integrated into product development and when the next CAB meeting will occur.

By following these guidelines, you can ensure your CAB meetings are not only effective but also provide significant value to both the participants and your organization, reinforcing the critical role CABs play in your customer engagement strategy.

Step 4: Follow-up on Customer Advisory Boards

Following a CAB meeting, effective follow-up actions are essential to capitalize on the momentum generated and to cement the value of the session for all participants. Here's a comprehensive guide to ensure the post-meeting process enhances customer relationships and drives continual improvement.

Finalize and Distribute Action Items

- **Action Item Compilation:** Quickly compile and finalize a list of action items identified during the meeting. This should include who is responsible for each item and the deadlines for completion.

- **Sharing of Materials:** Collect and distribute all presentations, meeting minutes, and detailed action items to all participants to ensure everyone has access to the same information and can reference discussions accurately.

Measure Success of the Advisory Council

- **Establish Success Metrics**: Define clear metrics for evaluating the success of the CAB at the planning stage. Ensure these metrics are focused on advice quality, depth of customer engagement, and relationship enhancement rather than sales.

- **Evaluate and Report**: Regularly assess the impact of the CAB on product development and customer satisfaction. Share these evaluations with CAB members to demonstrate the tangible benefits of their contributions and the direct impact of their advice on product improvements.

- **Member Rotation and Refresh**: To maintain a dynamic and effective CAB, periodically review the composition of the board. Introduce new members to bring fresh perspectives and expertise and rotate out members where necessary to align with evolving strategic goals.

After the Meeting Actions

- **Gather and Analyze Feedback**: Request and review feedback survey results to gauge the meeting's effectiveness and identify areas for improvement.

- **Document and Communicate**: Prepare a comprehensive post-event summary that captures the essence of the meeting including council highlights, lessons learned, and defined next steps. Share this summary along with a link to a shared drive folder containing all relevant documentation such as the agenda, registration list, and customer feedback.

- **Ongoing Documentation and Sharing**: Ensure that all council documents, including the attendee list, company and customer presentations (subject to confidentiality agreements), meeting minutes, and the action items list, are uploaded to the collaboration tool within one week after the meeting.

- **Sustain Engagement**: Continue to engage CAB members through online calls in-between CAB meetings or the collaboration tool by regularly updating them on the progress of action items and any new developments related to the council's discussions. Optionally, schedule a call with CAB members to review the progress of action items and discuss any immediate feedback or follow-up questions that may have arisen post-meeting.

By diligently following these follow-up steps, you not only reinforce the value of the CAB to its members but also ensure that the insights gained are effectively integrated into your strategic processes, leading to improved products and stronger customer relationships.

Step 5: Leverage Customer Advisory Boards for Product Success

In the journey of holistic product management, Customer Advisory Boards (CABs) play a pivotal role not just in gathering feedback but also in enhancing product success through strategic engagements. By leveraging the insights, engagement, and advocacy cultivated through CABs, you can significantly enhance your product's market position, customer satisfaction, and overall business outcomes.

This final step of the CAB cookbook focuses on how to effectively utilize the insights, relationships, and opportunities cultivated through CABs to boost your product's market performance and strategic alignment.

Define/Refine Product Strategy and Roadmap

Swiftly act on the insights and recommendations gathered from CAB meetings. Align these insights with your product development and strategic planning to ensure they influence business outcomes.

- **Feedback Integration**: Incorporate the actionable insights from CAB meetings into your product strategy and roadmap. This ensures that the voice of the customer is at the heart of your product planning.

- **Iterative Development**: Use CAB feedback to drive iterative improvements, ensuring that each development cycle is informed by real-world customer experiences and needs.

Let's delve into a couple of real-world examples that showcase the power of Customer Advisory Boards:

> **Story 1: The Feature Nobody Saw Coming**
>
> A leading software company established a CAB to gather feedback on a new marketing automation tool. While the discussions focused on expected features, the CAB members surprised everyone by highlighting their biggest struggle – data overload. This unexpected insight led to the development of an entirely new feature – an AI-powered data analysis tool – that became a game-changer for the product's success.
>
> **Story 2: The Pivot that Saved the Day**
>
> A company was developing a productivity app specifically for freelancers. Through CAB discussions, they discovered a crucial blind spot – their target audience also included busy corporate teams. By pivoting their focus to cater to a broader market segment, they were able to significantly improve the app's appeal and reach.

Cultivating Strong Customer References and Testimonials

CAB members, by virtue of their engagement and investment in your product's success, are prime candidates for generating powerful customer references and testimonials. These testimonials are not merely accolades but pivotal marketing tools that can dramatically reduce customer acquisition costs and increase the perceived value of your products. You can find more details in chapter 6 Amplifying Product Success Through Customer References and Testimonials.

- **Cultivate Advocacy**: Encourage CAB members to share their success stories and experiences. These narratives can be developed into powerful case studies and testimonials that highlight the value of your product, enhancing credibility and attracting new customers.
- **Utilize Feedback for Co-Innovation**: Use the collaborative relationships formed in CABs to drive co-innovation projects. These initiatives not only improve the product but also demonstrate to CAB members that their input has a direct and impactful contribution.

Internal Feedback Communication

- **Share Key Takeaways**: After each CAB meeting, share the key takeaways, feedback, and lessons learned with relevant internal teams. This ensures that the insights gathered are utilized effectively to align product strategies and customer service initiatives with customer expectations.
- **Engage Stakeholders**: Include product development, marketing, sales, and customer success teams in these reviews to foster a holistic understanding of customer needs and expectations.
- **Executive Summaries:** Prepare concise reports for senior management detailing the strategic insights and potential business impacts derived from CAB meetings. This keeps executives informed and engaged with the customer feedback process.
- **Internal Updates**: Regularly update internal stakeholders on CAB feedback and the progress of action items. This transparency helps in maintaining alignment and momentum across teams.

External Communication

- **External Updates**: Share presentations, meeting minutes, and additional information with CAB members and the broader customer community. Keeping customers informed demonstrates your commitment to their feedback and fosters continued engagement.

- **Quarterly Update Calls**: Schedule regular update calls with CAB members to keep them informed about progress, solicit ongoing feedback, and maintain strong relationships.

Measuring the Impact of CABs

- **Define Success Metrics Early**: Establish clear metrics at the planning stage to evaluate the CAB's effectiveness. These should focus on the quality of engagement, the relevance of the feedback to product improvements, and enhancements in customer relationships.

- **Assess CAB Influence on Product Success**: Regularly evaluate how CAB insights have led to better product-market fit, increased customer satisfaction, or influenced product strategy adjustments.

The power of Customer Advisory Boards lies in their ability to transform high-value customers into genuine product advocates and advisors. By effectively leveraging the insights and relationships developed through CABs, organizations can achieve:

- **Reduced Customer Acquisition Costs**: Through advocacy and testimonials that enhance brand credibility and attract new customers organically.

- **Increased Customer Lifetime Value**: As engaged customers are more likely to expand their use of your products and services.

- **Enhanced Product-Market Fit**: By ensuring that product developments are closely aligned with actual customer needs and market demands.

- **Boosted Company Valuation**: Through strong customer relationships and proven market engagement strategies.

By integrating CAB outcomes into your strategic planning and maintaining an active and responsive dialogue with CAB members, you can transform customer engagement into a robust driver of business success and product excellence.

Summary and Key Takeaways

This chapter has provided a comprehensive, step-by-step guide to establishing and managing a successful Customer Advisory Board (CAB). Through a detailed "CAB Cookbook," we have laid out a practical blueprint for creating both Executive Advisory Boards and Product-centric CABs that effectively align with your strategic objectives.

Here are the key takeaways that will help you ensure your CAB not only meets but surpasses its goals, delivering substantial value to your product, organization, and career:

Engagement and Impact

- Effective CABs foster deep, two-way engagement between your company and its most strategic customers.

- This engagement provides invaluable insights that directly influence product strategy and business growth, helping to align your offerings more closely with market needs and customer expectations.

Structured Approach

- Following a structured approach to planning, executing, and following up on CAB activities is crucial to maximize the benefits of your advisory board.

- Detailed planning includes defining clear objectives, selecting the right members, crafting thoughtful agendas, and executing engaging meetings that provide real value to participants.

Continuous Improvement

- Regular assessment and refinement of CAB processes and membership are essential to adapt to changing market conditions and evolving business objectives.

- Continuously enhance the structure and output of the CAB by incorporating feedback from board members and adjusting to new strategic insights.

Actionable Steps

- **Assess Needs**: Continuously evaluate both internal and external needs for a CAB to ensure it remains relevant and aligned with strategic goals.

- **Plan Thoroughly**: Detail every aspect of CAB operations, from member selection and communication strategies to meeting agendas and logistics.

- **Execute Effectively**: Conduct meetings that respect members' time and contribute significant value to their business and strategic interests.

- **Follow Up Rigorously**: Implement changes based on CAB feedback, monitor the impact of these changes, and communicate outcomes and new actions back to CAB members to maintain engagement and demonstrate the value of their contributions.

By adhering to these principles, you'll not only maintain a vibrant and effective CAB but also harness critical customer insights that can propel your product and company forward in the competitive market. This holistic approach to customer engagement through CABs ensures that your product management practices are deeply customer-centric, leading to improved product offerings and stronger customer relationships.

Moving Forward

As you continue to refine and expand your CAB initiatives, remember that the success of such boards hinges on your commitment to genuine engagement, strategic alignment, and the continuous loop of feedback and improvement. The insights gathered here should serve as a cornerstone for future endeavors in customer advocacy and strategic advisory, helping you to build a robust foundation for sustained business success and customer loyalty.

Customer Advisory Board (CAB) Project Plan (Template)

Whether you're planning your first CAB meeting or looking to refine your approach, this CAB Project Plan template will equip you with a jumpstart approach needed for success.

Project Plan Overview

- **Project Title**: [Name of the CAB Meeting]

- **Project Manager**: [Project Manager's Name]

- **Location**: [Venue Name, City]

- **Date**: [Meeting Date e.g. September 15.-16., 2025]

- **Overall Goals**: [State the primary goals of the CAB meeting]

Task Breakdown
Initial Planning & Coordination

- **Define Objectives and Scope**:
  - Tasks: Identify key goals, topics, and meeting format.
  - Responsible: [Product Lead, Project Manager]

- **Secure Venue and Logistics**:
  - Tasks: Book venue, catering, audio-visual, travel logistics, and accommodations.
  - Responsible: [Event Coordinator, Travel Team]

- **Create Budget & Financial Plan**:
    - Tasks: Estimate and allocate costs for venue, logistics, marketing, and customer travel.

- **Identify Key Stakeholders**:
    - Tasks: Form project team, designate roles, and finalize stakeholders.
    - Responsible: [Project Manager]

Task	Responsible	April 2026 CAB Deadline	September 2025 CAB Deadline
Define Objectives and Scope	[Product Lead, Project Manager]	November 15, 2025	April 15, 2025
Identify Key Stakeholders	[Project Manager]	November 15, 2025	April 15, 2025
Create Budget & Financial Plan	[Finance Team, Project Manager]	November 30, 2025	April 30, 2025
Secure Venue and Logistics	[Event Coordinator, Travel Team]	December 15, 2025	May 15, 2025

Recruitment & Invitations

- **Identify & Recruit CAB Members**:
    - Tasks: Shortlist potential candidates and reach out with personalized invitations.
    - Responsible: [Product Manager, Sales Team]
    - Deadline: [Deadline Date]

- **Distribute Save the Date Invitations**:
    - Tasks: Send initial "Save the Date" emails and follow up with formal invitations.
    - Responsible: [Marketing, Project Manager]

- **Confirm Attendance & Logistics**:
    - Tasks: Manage RSVP responses and handle customer travel arrangements.
    - Responsible: [Event Coordinator, Travel Team]

Task	Responsible	April 2026 CAB Deadline	September 2025 CAB Deadline
Identify & Recruit CAB Members	[Product Manager, Sales Team]	December 31, 2025	May 1, 2025
Distribute Save the Date Invitations	[Marketing, Project Manager]	January 15, 2026	June 15, 2025
Confirm Attendance & Logistics	[Event Coordinator, Travel Team]	March 15, 2026	August 15, 2025

Agenda Creation & Content Preparation

- **Draft Agenda & Meeting Structure**:

    - Tasks: Outline the meeting agenda, topics, and session formats. Check chapter CAB Agenda Template, Best Practices, and Examples.

    - Responsible: [Project Manager, Product Lead]

- **Secure Speakers & Panelists**:

    - Tasks: Confirm internal and external speakers/panelists and prepare briefing materials.

    - Responsible: [Project Manager, Product Lead]

- **Prepare Presentations & Materials**:

    - Tasks: Create slide decks, handouts, and any other meeting materials.

    - Responsible: [Marketing, Product Lead]

Task	Responsible	April 2026 CAB Deadline	September 2025 CAB Deadline
Draft Agenda & Meeting Structure	[Project Manager, Product Lead]	February 1, 2026	July 1, 2025
Secure Speakers & Panelists	[Project Manager, Product Lead]	February 15, 2026	July 15, 2025
Prepare Presentations & Materials	[Marketing, Product Lead]	March 15, 2026	August 15, 2025

Execution & Follow-Up

- **Event Setup & Execution**:

- Tasks: Set up venue, manage registration, and coordinate onsite logistics.

- Responsible: [Event Coordinator, Project Manager]

- **Feedback Collection & Follow-Up**:

    - Tasks: Conduct post-event surveys, debrief with stakeholders, and share insights with the team.

    - Responsible: [Marketing, Project Manager]

- **Action Item Review & Planning**:

    - Tasks: Outline key decisions and assign action items to relevant stakeholders.

    - Responsible: [Product Lead, Project Manager]

Task	Responsible	April 2026 CAB Deadline	September 2025 CAB Deadline
Event Setup & Execution	[Event Coordinator, Project Manager]	Day of Event 15. - 16. April	Day of Event 15. - 16. September
Feedback Collection & Follow-Up	[Marketing, Project Manager]	April 30, 2026	September 30, 2025
Action Item Review & Planning	[Product Lead, Project Manager]	May 15, 2026	October 15, 2025

Use this template to ensure that every aspect of your Customer Advisory Board meeting is meticulously planned and executed, from initial coordination to final follow-up, for a truly impactful customer engagement experience.

CAB Agenda Template, Best Practices, and Examples

A well-structured CAB agenda is essential to ensure these meetings are productive, engaging, and aligned with both your company's strategic vision and your customers' needs. In this chapter, we will explore best practices for crafting a compelling CAB agenda, provide a template to streamline your planning process, and share examples to inspire your approach. Whether you're planning your first CAB meeting or looking to refine your approach, these best practices, templates, and examples will equip you with the tools needed for success.

Core Agenda Components

- **Welcome & Networking**: Create a welcoming environment to build rapport among members.

- **Product Roadmap Update**: Begin with an overview of the product's current status and future direction.

- **Networking Time**: Include ample opportunities for informal relationship-building.

- **Workshops and Breakout Sessions**: Include interactive sessions where customers can discuss challenges and contribute ideas directly.

- **Customer Success Stories**: Highlight customer share-outs to build engagement and inspire peers.

- **Action Items**: Conclude with a recap of decisions made, along with a plan for follow-up activities.

- **Closing Remarks**: Summarize key takeaways and introduce the next interaction (virtual update meetings, next CAB, etc.).

Additional Agenda Options

- **Customer Share-Outs**: Invite customers to present their success stories, product use cases, or challenges and solicit peer feedback.

- **Market Analysis or Thought Leadership Session**: Share market trends or industry insights to stimulate strategic thinking.

- **Panel Discussions**: Organize panels with subject matter experts to address common challenges or emerging opportunities.

- **Product Demos**: Demonstrate new or upcoming features to provide a firsthand experience.

- **Innovation Challenges**: Invite members to brainstorm innovative solutions to specific challenges.

- **Q&A with Leadership**: Allocate time for members to ask candid questions of your executive team.

Illustrative 2-Day CAB Agenda Template
[Product Name] Customer Advisory Board Meeting Agenda

[Date] | [Location]

Day 1: Setting the Stage and Deep Engagement

TIME	ACTIVITY	DESCRIPTION	PRESENTER
8:00 AM 9:00 AM	Welcome & Networking Breakfast	Informal gathering to build rapport among members.	Facilitator
9:00 AM 9:30 AM	Opening Remarks	Introduction, goals for the meeting, and an overview of the agenda.	Facilitator or Product Lead
9:30 AM 10:30 AM	Product Strategy / Roadmap Update	Present the current status and future direction of the product.	Product Lead
10:30 AM 11:00 AM	Break	Networking opportunity.	-
11:00 AM 12:30 PM	Customer Share-Outs	Customers present success stories, use cases, and challenges.	Customer
12:30 PM 1:30 PM	Lunch	Informal networking over lunch.	-
1:30 PM 3:00 PM	Workshops & Breakout Sessions	Interactive sessions to discuss specific challenges and gather feedback.	Facilitator, PM assigned to each breakout
3:00 PM 3:30 PM	Break	Refreshments and networking.	-
3:30 PM 5:00 PM	Innovation Challenge	Brainstorming innovative solutions to specific challenges.	Facilitator, PM assigned to each topic
5:00 PM 5:30 PM	Closing Remarks	Summary of the day, key takeaways, and prep for Day 2.	Facilitator or Product Lead
6:00 PM 8:00 PM	Dinner & Networking Event	Informal evening gathering to build relationships.	-

Day 2: Deep Dives and Strategic Alignment

TIME	ACTIVITY	DESCRIPTION	PRESENTER
8:00 AM 9:00 AM	Breakfast & Networking	Informal gathering to start the day.	Facilitator
9:00 AM 9:30 AM	Recap of Day 1	Review key takeaways and set the stage for Day 2.	Facilitator or Product Lead
9:30 AM 10:30 AM	Market Analysis / Thought Leadership Session	Share market trends or industry insights.	Product Marketing or External Thought Leader
10:30 AM 11:00 AM	Break	Networking opportunity.	-
11:00 AM 12:30 PM	Panel Discussion	Subject matter experts address common challenges or emerging opportunities.	Customers, Product, Partners, Industry Experts
12:30 PM 1:30 PM	Lunch	Informal networking over lunch.	-
1:30 PM 3:00 PM	Product Demos	Demonstrate new or upcoming features for hands-on experience.	Product / Pre-Sales team
3:00 PM 3:30 PM	Break	Refreshments and networking.	-
3:30 PM 4:30 PM	Q&A with Leadership	Open floor for members to ask candid questions to the executive team.	Facilitator or Product Lead
4:30 PM 5:00 PM	Closing Remarks & Action Items	Summarize key takeaways, action items, and next steps.	Facilitator or Product Lead
5:00 PM 5:30 PM	Informal Networking	Final opportunity to connect before departing.	-

Best Practices

- **Clarity of Purpose**: Clearly communicate the purpose and goals of the CAB to all members.

- **Balanced Agenda**: Provide a mix of presentations, breakout sessions, and networking opportunities to keep members engaged. Mix structured sessions with networking opportunities to foster relationship-building.

- **Diversity of Sessions**: Mix different session types (presentations, workshops, and panels) to keep participants engaged. Introduce new elements at each meeting to keep the format fresh and engaging.

- **Customer-Centric**: Tailor the agenda to address the interests and pain points of the attending members. Involve CAB members in agenda setting by asking for their input and interests beforehand.

- **Time Management**: Monitor time closely to ensure sessions remain focused and run according to schedule.

- **Follow-Up**: Ensure timely follow-up on action items and maintain ongoing communication between meetings.

- **Feedback Loop**: Regularly seek feedback from members on the meeting structure and content to refine future sessions.

- **Non-Sales Focus**: Keep the meeting agenda focused on strategic discussions rather than sales pitches.

Example Agenda: First CAB Meeting for Single Product
Agenda – Day 1
Wednesday, Sept 25th, 2024 – Meeting Room: Advocacy

Time	Description	Facilitator / Presenter	Duration
19:00 sept 24th	Dinner	Company Team + Customers	
08:00 – 08:15	Welcome / Agenda Review / Meeting Objectives	Product Lead	15 min
08:15 – 9:35	Customer Introductions – First Round (8 Customer x 10min)	Customer Advisory Council Members	80 min
9:35 – 10:00	Break & Networking		25 min
10:00 – 11:20	Introductions – Second Round (8 Customer x 10min)	Customer Advisory Council Members	
11:20 – 12:20	Recent Innovations and Roadmap – Part 1	Product team	60 min
12:20 – 13:00	Lunch & Emails		40 min
13:00 – 14:00	Recent Innovations and Roadmap – Part 2	Product team	60 min
14:00 – 14:20	Customer YOUR PRODUCT Journey I	Selected Customer Member	20 min
14:40 – 15:00	Customer YOUR PRODUCT Journey II	Selected Customer Member	20 min
	Break & Networking		20 min
15:00 – 15:30	Recent Innovations and Roadmap – Part 3	Product team	30 min
15:30 – 16:15	Workshop – Strategic Priorities in YOUR PRODUCT Team 1 – Topic 1 (Lead: TBD &TBD) Team 2 – Topic 2 (Lead: TBD &TBD) Team 3 – Topic 3 (Lead: TBD &TBD)	Product & Customer Advisory Council Members	75 min
16:15 – 16:30	What is next?	Product Lead	15 min
19:00	Team Dinner	All	

Example Agenda: Established CAB for Product Line

Monday, April 3rd

Time	Topic	Presenter
1:00 p.m.	Registration	
1:30 p.m.	Opening and Welcome	Product Lead
2:00 p.m.	<Your Product> – Release Preview – Module 1 • Feature / Customer Job 1 • Feature / Customer Job 2 • Feature / Customer Job 3 • Feature / Customer Job 4	Product team
3:30 p.m.	Coffee Break	
4:00 p.m.	<Your Product> – Release Preview – Module 2 • Feature / Customer Job 1 • Feature / Customer Job 2 • Feature / Customer Job 3 • Feature / Customer Job 4 • Feature / Customer Job 5 • Feature / Customer Job 6	Product team
6:00 p.m.	End of Day 1	

Tuesday, April 4th

Time	Topic	Presenter
9:00 a.m.	Recap day 1	Product Lead
9:15 a.m.	<Your Product> – Release Preview – Product 1 • Feature / Customer Job 1 • Feature / Customer Job 2 • Feature / Customer Job 3	Product team
10:15 p.m.	Coffee Break	
10:45 a.m.	The Journey of <Your Product> at Customer A	Customer representative
11:45 a.m.	<Your Product> Embedded in the Bigger Picture	Product Lead
12:45 p.m.	Lunch	
1:45 p.m.	<Your Product> – break-out sessions on specific topics Topics have been crowdsourced and prioritized with CAB before • Topic 1 • Topic 2 • Topic 3 • Topic 4 • ...	All
4:00 p.m.	Discuss results of break-out sessions	All
6:00 p.m.	Leave for Dinner	

Wednesday, April 5th

Time	Topic	Presenter
9:00 a.m.	Recap day 2	Product Lead
9:15 a.m.	Case Study of <Your Product> at Customer B	Customer B representative
10:15 a.m.	Coffee break	
10:45 a.m.	Partner product showcase	Partner A
11:45 a.m.	Partner product showcase	Partner B
12:45 p.m.	Lunch	
2:00 p.m.	Partner product showcase	Partner C
3:00 p.m.	Update on Customer Loyalty Program	Engagement Manager
3:30 p.m.	Wrap-up	Product Lead
4:00 p.m.	End of CAB Meeting	

By applying these strategies and best practices, companies can establish Customer Advisory Boards that deliver valuable insights, foster deep customer relationships, and ultimately shape a more customer-centric product strategy.

Templates: Communication Types and Best Practices

Save the Date Invitation Template

Subject: Save the Date for Our Upcoming [Product Name] Customer Advisory Board Meeting

"""

Dear [First Name],

We are thrilled to announce our next Customer Advisory Board meeting, scheduled for [Month, Day, Year], in [Location]. This exclusive event is designed to bring together our strategic partners like you to collaborate on shaping the future of [Product Name].

Please mark your calendar for this invaluable opportunity to exchange insights, share your expertise, and contribute to the [Product Name] vision. A formal invitation with more details will follow.

Warm Regards,

[Your Signature]

"""

Best Practices and Tips:

- **Timing**: Send out 4-5 months before the event to give attendees ample notice.

- **Details**: Include the date, location, and the collaborative nature of the meeting.

- **Encouragement**: Highlight why their input matters and how their participation impacts the product strategy and innovation agenda.

- **Personalization:** Address the customer directly and acknowledge their importance.
- **Purpose:** Clearly state the event's collaborative nature to encourage participation.

Invite to Collaboration Group Template

Subject: Join the Exclusive [Product Name] Customer Advisory Board Collaboration Group

""

Dear [First Name],

As a valuable member of our Customer Advisory Board, we're excited to invite you to join our exclusive [Collaboration Platform Name] group.

This space allows you to:

- Access the latest meeting agendas, presentations, and materials.
- Share your insights and connect with fellow CAB members.
- Participate in ongoing discussions that help shape the [Product Name] strategy and innovation agenda.

Join now: [add Collaboration Group Link]

We're eager to hear your valuable input in the group!

Best Regards,

[Your Signature]

""

Best Practices and Tips:

- **Accessibility**: Make the collaboration platform user-friendly and provide clear instructions for joining. Use the same technology for all CABs (EAC, CAB, Working Groups)

- **Engagement**: Highlight the collaborative nature of the group and how members can make an impact.

- **Benefits:** Emphasize how sharing knowledge and ideas benefits both the individual and the broader community.

CAB Membership Invitation Template

Subject: Invitation to Join Our [Product Name] Customer Advisory Board

"""

Dear [First Name],

We're excited to extend an exclusive invitation for you to join our [Product Name] Customer Advisory Board. As a CAB member, you will:

- Collaborate directly with product leadership to shape the future of [Product Name].
- Network with other industry leaders who share your commitment to innovation.
- Provide feedback that influences our roadmap and business strategy.

We believe your expertise and perspective will be invaluable in helping us elevate [Product Name].

Please confirm your interest by [RSVP Deadline]. We look forward to welcoming you!

Sincerely,

[Your Signature]

"""

Best Practices and Tips:

- **Personalization**: Tailor the invitation to the specific customer.

- **Value Proposition**: Clearly state the benefits of joining the CAB and how it aligns with their interests.

CAB Meeting Invitation Template

Subject: Official Invitation: [Product Name] Customer Advisory Board Meeting

""

Dear [First Name],

We are delighted to formally invite you to the [Product Name] Customer Advisory Board meeting on [Month, Day, Year], in [Location].

This meeting will feature:

- *Strategic updates on the product roadmap and vision.*
- *Collaborative workshops to discuss your challenges and goals.*
- *Networking opportunities with fellow leaders and experts.*

Please RSVP by [RSVP Deadline] to secure your spot and hotel accommodations.

Warm Regards,

[Your Signature]

""

Best Practices & Tips:

- **RSVP Deadline**: Clearly state the deadline for confirming attendance.
- **Logistics**: Provide comprehensive details on the venue, travel, and accommodations.
- **Agenda Highlights**: Include high-level topics to spark interest.

5 Completing the Customer Advocacy Pyramid

Introduction

The Customer Advocacy Pyramid is not just a model but a dynamic framework that incorporates diverse strategies to engage customers at every level. By fully understanding and implementing each component, Product Managers can ensure that their products not only meet but exceed the evolving needs of their users, driving growth through deepened customer relationships and sustained advocacy. This holistic approach is fundamental in today's competitive market, where customer loyalty and proactive engagement are paramount.

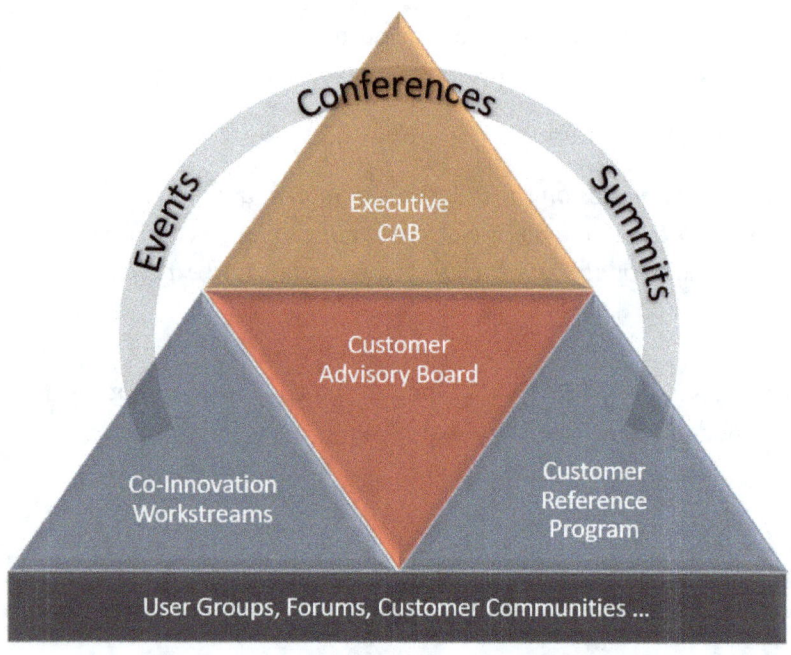

Figure 7: The Customer Advocacy Pyramid

Establishing Co-Innovation Workstreams

As we've explored in previous chapters, Customer Advisory Boards (CABs) form the central component of the Customer Advocacy Pyramid, providing a solid foundation for strategic customer engagement and insight gathering.

Let's build on that foundation, introducing Co-Innovation Workstreams as pivotal elements that leverage CABs to foster deeper product innovation through customer collaboration. Co-Innovation Workstreams are integral to the Customer Advocacy Pyramid, serving as the bridge between customer feedback and actionable product improvements. These workstreams initiate out of CABs and directly involve customers and company teams in developing new solutions or enhancing existing products, driven by co-creation efforts.

The insights and outcomes from these collaborative projects are not only shared back with CAB members but also highlighted at Executive Advisory Boards, Events, or Conferences, ensuring a continuous loop of feedback and innovation.

Co-Innovation Workstreams are dynamic collaborative projects that integrate directly with the structure of Customer Advisory Boards. These workstreams harness the expertise and insights of CAB members to tackle specific product challenges or explore new opportunities through deep, tactical engagement.

Structure and Functioning

- **Integration with CABs**: Co-Innovation Workstreams are directly spawned from discussions and needs identified in CAB meetings, ensuring that the topics addressed are highly relevant and of strategic importance.

- **Cross-functional Collaboration**: These sessions involve cross-disciplinary teams from both the customer side and the company, including product managers, developers, and customer success specialists. For these topic-related advisory streams, it's optimal to include at least three but no more than five companies. This size is ideal for facilitating easier consensus-building and ensures that discussions remain focused and productive.

- **Host/Sponsor**: Typically led by a Product Manager, who ensures that the workstream's goals align with the overall product strategy and the specific needs of the participants.

- **Feedback Loop**: Continuous feedback during these sessions helps refine ideas and solutions in real-time, which are then fed back into the broader CAB discussions for further validation and refinement. Key to these sessions is the interactive exchange of ideas and feedback, which helps prioritize customer needs and align them with product innovations. The Product Manager uses these sessions to ideate and validate innovations, leveraging direct input from key users to shape the product's future.

- **Meeting Frequency and Duration**: Workstreams may meet more frequently during intensive development phases, combining in-person group sessions, one-on-one meetings, and virtual discussions. Meetings typically span 1-2 days, focusing intensively on the predefined topics.

Benefits

- **Executive and Customer Advisory Board Value:** Results and progress are regularly reported back to the entire CAB and may also be showcased in larger forums such as Executive Advisory Boards or annual customer conferences, enhancing transparency and collective engagement.

- **Accelerated Innovation:** By focusing on co-creation, these workstreams can rapidly iterate on ideas and prototypes, significantly speeding up the innovation process.

- **Enhanced Customer Buy-in:** Customers involved in these workstreams often develop a deeper commitment to the product's success, as they see their input directly influencing the product development. By engaging deeply on specific issues, these workstreams can quickly move from conceptual discussions to practical, implementable solutions.

- **Richer Product Insights:** The diverse perspectives gathered through these collaborative efforts enrich the product's alignment with market needs and customer expectations.

- **Enhanced Customer Relations**: Participants often feel a greater sense of involvement and ownership over the product roadmap, fostering stronger loyalty and long-term engagement.

User Groups, Communities, and Meet-Ups

User groups, communities, and meet-ups form an essential tier within the Customer Advocacy Pyramid. These platforms allow users to connect, share experiences, and grow together, fostering a robust ecosystem around the product.

User groups, communities, and meet-ups are often user-driven, providing a grassroots level of engagement where real-world use cases and challenges can be discussed openly. They offer a support network for users, facilitating knowledge exchange and problem-solving, which enhances user competence and confidence in the product. Regular meet-ups and community forums provide continuous engagement opportunities, keeping users connected to the product team and each other.

In-person User Groups: Facilitate or encourage the formation of both in-person and online user groups focused on your product or service.

- **Approach:** Provide resources, seed topics for discussion, and consider offering moderation for both official and self-organized groups.
- **Benefits:** Creates a sense of belonging, fosters knowledge sharing, and provides a direct line for collecting customer feedback.
- **Challenges:** Requires some initial investment in set-up and potential moderation of discussions, especially with more technical products.

Online User Groups: Online user groups centered around your product foster connection and learning.

- **Approach:** Provide resources for both, moderate online spaces, and consider "hybrid" events with streaming elements for wider reach.
- **Benefits:** Creates a vibrant community, provides multiple avenues for knowledge sharing, and offers ongoing access to valuable customer insights.
- **Challenges:** Maintaining engagement in both spheres, finding a balance between in-person and online investment.

Hybrid or virtual Meet-ups (Local Impact, Global Reach) Organize informal gatherings focusing on knowledge exchange and networking.

- **Approach:** Partner with local advocates, host hybrid in-person and pure virtual meet-ups and promote online to boost awareness of upcoming sessions.

- **Benefits:** Builds community spirit, reinforces brand loyalty, and allows for targeted discussions based on location or need.
- **Challenges:** Juggling logistics of physical events alongside online components, ensuring virtual options are equally engaging.

Local Meet-ups: Organize informal gatherings, either locally or regionally, focusing on knowledge exchange and networking around your product.

- **Approach:** Partner with local advocates, provide venues or host virtual meet-ups, offer light refreshments, and focus on valuable content or experience sharing.
- **Benefits:** Builds community, reinforces brand loyalty, and generates valuable insights directly from users.
- **Challenges:** Logistics and costs for in-person events, ensuring meet-ups remain focused and offer value, rather than solely becoming promotional.

Moving beyond formal structures, user groups, communities, and meet-ups represent the grassroots level of customer engagement within the Customer Advocacy Pyramid. These platforms allow for informal yet meaningful exchanges between users, fostering a sense of community and collective learning.

Strategic Importance:

- **Feedback Mechanism:** Regular interactions with user communities provide continuous feedback streams, which are invaluable for ongoing product improvements. They act as informal feedback channels, where spontaneous discussions can yield insights that may not surface in more structured settings.
- **Advocacy and Loyalty:** Engaged users are more likely to become product advocates, sharing their positive experiences within their professional networks and contributing to the product's market reputation. Regular meet-ups and online interactions help build a strong community of advocates who support and promote the product organically.
- **Support and Knowledge Exchange:** These groups provide a supportive environment where users can share challenges, solutions, and hacks related to the product.

PM Role and Support Functions:

- **Strategic Oversight:** The Product Manager ensures that community feedback is integrated into the product development lifecycle, aligning user insights with strategic product goals.

- **Supporting Functions:** Marketing and customer success teams play crucial roles in facilitating these communities, providing resources, organizing meet-ups, and ensuring that community feedback is systematically captured and acted upon.

Lights on – Showcase Customer Engagement and Advocacy

Strategically scheduling conferences and summits around major industry events can maximize attendance and reduce travel, contributing to sustainability goals. These events serve as pivotal moments to gather testimonials, showcase co-innovation successes, and strengthen customer relationships in a dynamic, engaging environment.

Company Conferences & Events: Hosting a dedicated conference for your customer and user base creates a powerful shared experience.

- **Approach:** Engage keynote speakers from your customer base, industry experts, analysts, and your own organization, consider product workshops, networking opportunities, and social events. Livestream key components and make content accessible afterwards for wider reach.
- **Benefits:** Strengthens customer relationships, demonstrates appreciation, can be a source of new leads, and provides a platform to unveil new features or strategic shifts, and can drive significant buzz both online and off.
- **Challenges:** Significant time and financial investment in planning and execution. Your competitors will have their eyes and ears wide open.

Industry Events & Summits: Optimize your participation in relevant industry trade shows, summits, and conferences.

- **Approach:** Sponsor events, secure speaking opportunities, have a well-designed booth to attract engagement, and network with key decision-makers and potential customers. Create pre- and post-event online buzz through social media or dedicated campaigns.
- **Benefits:** Raises brand awareness, facilitates lead generation, positions your company as a thought leader, and offers opportunities for competitive analysis.
- **Challenges:** Standing out in a crowded marketplace. Ensuring your presence generates tangible results, not just participation. Ensuring both online and in-person efforts are cohesive and not isolated.

B2B vs. B2C Environment Considerations

B2B Environment: Prioritize industry events with targeted audiences, leverage online tools like webinar and hybrid or local meet-ups, personalize your engagement to address specific pain points, and leverage CABs for strategic guidance and thought leadership.

B2C Environment: Community-driven events and user groups are particularly powerful, foster brand loyalty through shared experiences, and leverage social media to drive meet-up participation. Tap into social media platforms, foster vibrant online communities, and create shareable content driven by community participation.

Key Takeaways

By integrating these elements into your customer engagement strategy, you can ensure a comprehensive approach that not only focuses on gathering insights but also actively involves customers in the creation and refinement of your products. This holistic approach is crucial for driving innovation, enhancing customer satisfaction, and maintaining a competitive edge in today's fast-paced market environments.

- ✓ **Leverage Co-Innovation Workstreams**: Product leads and managers should actively leverage Co-Innovation Workstreams to harness customer insights for real-time product innovation. These collaborative projects not only drive product enhancements that are closely aligned with customer needs but also foster deeper engagement by involving customers directly in the development process.

- ✓ **Cultivate Strong Customer Relations**: By engaging customers through structured Co-Innovation Workstreams and informal user groups, product managers can build stronger, more meaningful relationships. These relationships are critical for developing a loyal customer base that is more likely to advocate for the product and contribute to sustained business growth. Face-to-face engagement offers unique opportunities to create genuine connections with customers.

- ✓ **Utilize User Groups for Continuous Feedback**: Establish and maintain active user groups to gather ongoing feedback, which is invaluable for iterative product improvements. These groups provide a platform for users to express their needs, preferences, and challenges, offering insights that may not emerge through formal channels.

- ✓ **Enhance Product Strategies with Diverse Insights**: Integrating diverse customer perspectives through Co-Innovation Workstreams and user communities can significantly enrich the product's alignment with market needs. Product leads should use these insights to refine their product strategies, ensuring they meet the evolving demands of the market.

- ✓ **Drive Product Adoption and Advocacy**: Engaging customers in co-innovation and community-building efforts not only enhances product features and usability but also increases customer satisfaction and loyalty. Satisfied customers are more likely to become advocates, helping to drive product adoption through their networks.

- ✓ **Implement a Holistic Engagement Approach**: Product managers should adopt a holistic approach to customer engagement, utilizing each layer of the Customer Advocacy Pyramid to maximize impact. This comprehensive approach ensures that all customer interactions—from high-level strategic discussions in CABs to informal exchanges in user groups—contribute to a cohesive strategy that drives product success and customer satisfaction. B2B and B2C audiences require tailored approaches when planning and executing customer engagement events.

By focusing on these key areas, product leads, and product managers can effectively use the Customer Advocacy Pyramid to enhance their product offerings, strengthen customer relationships, and drive significant business outcomes.

6 Amplifying Product Success Through Customer References and Testimonials

Introduction

In the realm of product management, the potency of customer references and testimonials cannot be overstated. These elements are not just add-ons to the marketing toolkit; they are essential components that drive product success and maintain market fit. This chapter delves into how leveraging Customer Advisory Boards (CABs) and community engagement can enrich your customer references, turning satisfied customers into powerful advocates who can enhance your brand's visibility and credibility.

The Strategic Importance of Customer References

Customer references and testimonials serve as invaluable assets in any sales and marketing strategy. They provide prospective customers with real-world evidence of your product's impact, helping to shorten sales cycles and improve market penetration. Furthermore, these references are critical for maintaining product-market fit by ensuring that your offerings continue to meet the evolving needs of your target audience.

In a digital age where consumers increasingly rely on the experiences of others to make purchasing decisions, customer references and testimonials have become crucial for business success. This chapter delves into the strategic utilization of customer references and testimonials, offering a roadmap to harness these powerful tools to enhance credibility, attract new customers, and ultimately drive growth.

Leveraging CABs for Dynamic Customer References

Customer Advisory Boards are fertile grounds for cultivating strong customer references. Members of these boards are typically highly engaged and invested in your product's success, making them ideal candidates for delivering compelling testimonials and participating in reference activities. Here's how to effectively use CABs for this purpose:

1. **Assess Customer Willingness and Readiness**:

- Engage with customers during or after positive trigger events (e.g., successful product deployment, requests for discounts, or other give-and-take scenarios) to gauge their interest in becoming a reference.

- Understand and respect their preferences for being an official or unofficial reference based on their company policies.

- Discuss various formats such as written references, videos, speaking engagements, or direct customer-to-customer calls.

2. **Collect Essential Reference Information**:

- Gather comprehensive information including company background, customer contact details, product usage, and significant achievements.

- Document challenges overcome by the customer, quantifiable benefits obtained through your product, and the customer's future plans.

3. **Build and Review References**:

- Use the collected data to craft compelling stories. Consider hiring professional writers or content creators to ensure high-quality output.

- Share drafts with internal stakeholders for feedback and iterate as necessary to refine the content.

- Obtain customer feedback and necessary approvals efficiently, using streamlined processes and tools like approval forms.

4. **Compliance and Documentation**:

- Adhere to relevant regulations such as GDPR when personal details are involved, ensuring all necessary consents are obtained.

- Document and catalogue the completed references for easy access and use in various go-to-market activities.

Structuring Your Customer Reference Approach

1. **Collection and Curation**

- **Identify Your Advocates**: Start with identifying satisfied customers who can articulate their positive experiences clearly. These are your potential advocates whose stories can resonate with your target audience.

- **Gather Diverse Testimonials**: Ensure a mix of testimonials that address different aspects of your product and come from various industries or user types to appeal to a broader audience.

- **Keep it Authentic**: Authenticity is key. Encourage customers to speak in their own words and avoid overly scripted testimonials.

2. **Leveraging Testimonials Effectively**

- **Website Placement**: Strategically place testimonials on your website where they can have the most impact, such as the homepage, product pages, or checkout pages.

- **Social Proof in Marketing**: Use testimonials in marketing campaigns, on social media, and in email newsletters to build trust and credibility.

- **Sales Enablement**: Arm your sales team with powerful customer stories that can help overcome objections and close deals.

3. **Creating Compelling Case Studies**

- **Choose the Right Stories**: Select customer stories that highlight significant challenges overcome or notable successes achieved with your product supporting your marketing messaging and value propositions.

- **Detail the Journey**: Outline the customer's initial challenges, the solutions provided by your product, and the outcomes. This narrative framework helps potential customers envision their success with your product.

- **Use Varied Formats**: Produce case studies in different formats, such as video, infographics, and long-form articles, to cater to different consumption preferences.

4. **Best Practices for Maintenance and Improvement**

- **Regular Updates**: Keep your testimonials and case studies current to reflect the evolving nature of your product and market.

- **Feedback Loops**: Use customer feedback not only for testimonials but also for insights into product improvements and innovation.

- **Quantify Results**: Where possible, include quantifiable achievements in your testimonials and case studies to provide clear evidence of your product's impact.

Integrating or Establishing Customer Loyalty Programs

Connecting customer references to a loyalty program can significantly enhance participation rates. Offer incentives such as free consulting hours, exclusive access to new products, or branded merchandise in exchange for their engagement as official references. Such programs not only encourage more customers to participate but also deepen their relationship with your brand, creating a cycle of continuous engagement and advocacy.

Utilizing Customer References

Once established, customer references should be actively used across various channels and platforms:

- **Sales Enablement**: Equip your sales teams with reference materials that can address potential customer concerns and accelerate the decision-making process.

- **Marketing Campaigns**: Feature customer testimonials in marketing materials, from digital content to print media, to build trust and authenticity.

- **Strategic Meetings**: Use customer success stories in strategic discussions and presentations to highlight product impact and market relevance.

Customer references and testimonials are not just marketing tools.

- They are genuine voices that can significantly influence perception and buying behavior.
- They provide prospective customers with real-world proof of your product's effectiveness and your company's commitment to customer satisfaction.
- They are a testament to a product's success and customer satisfaction.

By effectively leveraging the insights and advocacy generated through CABs and integrating them with customer loyalty initiatives, organizations can not only enhance their market positioning but also foster an environment of continuous improvement and customer-centric innovation.

The importance and the power of customer voices manifests the need to put it on your radar as part of Product&360 - the holistic approach to product management. This ensures that customer voices are not only heard but are also instrumental in shaping product success.

Key Takeaways for Effective Customer Reference Management

Creating and managing customer references is a strategic endeavor that necessitates a clear and systematic approach. Here are key takeaways to ensure that your customer references are impactful and align with your sales and marketing objectives.

Structured Reference Process

Collaborate with your sales and marketing leaders to develop a proactive, structured reference process. Establish clear criteria for when to accept or decline reference requests.

Understand what prospective customers seek from a reference and tailor your assets accordingly. Remember, it is perfectly acceptable to decline a reference request if it does not align with your strategic goals or if the quality of the reference may be compromised.

Quality Over Quantity

Focus on creating high-quality reference content that highlights the value and outcomes provided by your product. Avoid generic corporate language; instead, emphasize tangible benefits and measurable improvements that resonate with the specific needs of your business and IT stakeholders.

Strategic Use of References

Maintain an organized system for your references, categorizing them by market segments, regions, industries, customer sizes, and the age of the reference to quickly match them to prospective customer needs.

Prioritize the development of references that fill gaps in your portfolio and strategically invest time in those that will offer the highest return on engagement.

Timing and Necessity

Capitalize on trigger events to request references. These events can include a customer asking for a higher discount, going live successfully, or initiating a reference request themselves.

Recognize the effort required by customers to provide a reference and request them judiciously. Reserve your high-quality references for opportunities with the greatest potential impact.

Empower Your Teams

Educate your sales and marketing teams about the strategic importance of customer references. They should understand when to utilize these assets and how to effectively communicate their value to prospective customers.

The Power of Saying No

Use discretion in managing reference requests. If there's any doubt about the appropriateness or the potential impact of a reference, it's better to decline. Educating your teams about this selective approach will help preserve the integrity and effectiveness of your reference assets.

By adhering to these guidelines, you ensure that your customer references not only support your go-to-market strategies but also reinforce the credibility and trustworthiness of your product offerings. This approach will transform satisfied customers into compelling advocates, enhancing your competitive edge and contributing to sustained product success.

7 Measuring Success Across the Customer Advocacy Pyramid

Introduction

Understanding the efficacy of various components within the Customer Advocacy Pyramid is critical to ensuring that each segment contributes positively to the overall strategy of product management and customer engagement. This chapter provides a framework for evaluating the entire spectrum of the Customer Advocacy Pyramid, which includes Customer Advisory Boards (CABs), Co-Innovation Workstreams, User Groups, Communities, Meet-Ups, and the strategic use of customer references and testimonials. To ensure that your Customer Advisory Board (CAB) is not just operational but also successful and impactful, it is crucial to establish and follow clear metrics for its evaluation. These metrics should accurately reflect the CAB's objectives, focusing primarily on the quality of advice, the depth of customer engagement, and the enhancement of relationships.

Establishing Comprehensive Success Metrics

By clearly defining and rigorously measuring success metrics focused on the quality of advice, depth of engagement, and relationship enhancement, you can significantly amplify the impact of your Customer Engagement initiatives.

When setting metrics for evaluating the effectiveness of your customer engagement strategies, it's essential to capture a broad range of impacts:

Quality of Advisory Contributions:

- **Relevance**: Measure how the advice and feedback align with your strategic goals. This can be assessed through follow-up actions taken on the advice and the outcomes of those actions.
- **Innovativeness**: Evaluate the novelty and usefulness of the insights provided. Were there unique perspectives or solutions that came out of the CAB that you hadn't considered before?
- **Clarity and Actionability**: Assess how clear and actionable the advice given by the board members is. The more precise and implementable the feedback, the higher its quality.

- **Co-Innovation Outcomes**: Measure the practical impact of innovations developed through co-innovation workstreams, including adoption rates and user satisfaction.

Depth of Engagement

- **Participation Levels:** Monitor engagement across forums, including user groups and CAB meetings, noting active participation and dropout rates. Track attendance and participation levels in meetings and activities. High engagement levels are indicative of a valuable and well-regarded CAB.
- **Interaction Quality**: Evaluate the depth of discussions and the value of interactions within these communities. Analyze the depth and breadth of discussions. Are members actively discussing, debating, and engaging with the topics at hand?
- **Longevity of Engagement**: Monitor how long members stay engaged over multiple sessions and activities. Long-term engagement is a strong indicator of the CAB's relevance and value to its members.

Relationship Enhancement:
- **Net Promoter Score (NPS)**: Utilize NPS or similar metrics to gauge members' likelihood of recommending your company based on their CAB experience.
- **Customer Loyalty and Retention**: Measure changes in customer loyalty and retention rates among CAB members compared to non-members.
- **Trust and Satisfaction Levels**: Conduct regular assessments of trust and satisfaction among CAB members, focusing on their perceptions of how their feedback is being used and valued.

Advocacy and Loyalty:

- **Reference Rate of CAB Members**: Track how often CAB members act as references or advocates for your product.
- **Testimonials**: Quantify the testimonials generated through these engagements and assess their impact on prospective customers.
- **Community Health**: Measure the vibrancy and growth of user communities and meet-ups, looking at new memberships, retention rates, and overall activity levels.

Implementing the Measurement Process

To effectively measure these dimensions, consider the following practices:

Surveys and Feedback Loops: Deploy regular surveys and feedback mechanisms across all platforms to gauge satisfaction, collect qualitative feedback, and understand the community's health.

- **Surveys**: Regularly distribute surveys to CAB members to collect quantitative and qualitative data on their experiences and the perceived value of the CAB.
- **Interviews and Feedback Sessions**: Conduct periodic interviews or informal feedback sessions with CAB members to gather more detailed insights into their experiences and suggestions for improvement.

Analysis and Reporting: Compile data into actionable reports that highlight trends, successes, and areas needing attention. Utilize visual dashboards to maintain an ongoing view of key metrics.

- **Regular Reports**: Compile and review the collected data regularly to assess progress against the established metrics. Create detailed reports that highlight trends, successes, and areas for improvement.

- **Dashboarding**: Utilize visual dashboards to track key metrics over time. This helps in quickly identifying patterns and making informed decisions based on real-time data.

Continuous Engagement and Improvement: Use insights from data to improve community management strategies, refine CAB agendas, and enhance co-innovation processes.

- **Action Plans**: Develop action plans based on the metrics and feedback collected. Ensure these plans are communicated back to the CAB members to show how their input is being used.
- **Continuous Improvement**: Use the insights gained from the metrics to continuously refine CAB activities and interactions. This not only improves the effectiveness of the CAB but also demonstrates a commitment to valuing and acting on member input.

Leveraging CABs and Community Engagement for Powerful Customer References

- **Strategic Utilization of CAB Insights**: Transform insights from CAB discussions into compelling case studies and testimonials that highlight the effectiveness and impact of your products.
- **Community-Driven Content Creation**: Encourage user communities to share their success stories and experiences, which can be developed into testimonials or case studies.
- **Highlighting Co-Innovation Success**: Showcase successful co-innovation projects at industry events, in marketing materials, and through digital content platforms to demonstrate the practical benefits of customer collaboration.

Conclusion

Measuring the success of the components within the Customer Advocacy Pyramid provides a clear picture of how customer engagement strategies directly contribute to product success and market fit. By establishing robust metrics and regularly evaluating these engagements, product managers can not only enhance product offerings but also build a loyal customer base that actively supports and promotes their brand.

The strategic integration of CAB insights, community feedback, and customer testimonials into your marketing and product development processes ensures that your customer advocacy efforts yield tangible results. This holistic approach not only boosts customer satisfaction but also empowers customers to become brand advocates, thereby driving organic growth and enhancing your product's market presence.

This strategic approach not only helps in achieving specific product and business goals but also strengthens the overall relationship with key customers, ultimately driving long-term success and customer loyalty.

Through regular evaluation and adaptation based on the metrics outlined, you can ensure that Customer Engagement & Advocacy remains a valuable asset, continuously contributing to the company's objectives while enhancing customer satisfaction.

The consistent application of these metrics facilitates a cycle of continuous improvement, where insights from e.g. CAB sessions inform product strategies and business decisions, which in turn foster deeper customer relationships and more meaningful engagement. As you refine your approach based on these success measures, your customer engagement initiatives will evolve into a critical tool for customer-driven innovation and strategic alignment.

This proactive approach to customer engagement and advisory boards is what distinguishes leading companies in today's fast-paced business environment.

8 Harnessing the Power of Customer Personalities Across Engagement Platforms

Introduction

Understanding and leveraging the diverse personalities of customer participants is crucial for the success of any customer engagement initiative, whether it's an Executive Advisory Board (EAB), Customer Advisory Board (CAB), Co-Innovation Workstream, User Group, or when gathering Customer References/Testimonials. This chapter explores different customer personalities and offers strategies on how to effectively engage each type in various customer engagement formats.

Identifying Customer Personalities

Drawing on insights from customer engagement studies, including Forrester's analysis of advocate personalities, we can categorize customer personalities into four primary types:

1. **The Educator**: Enjoys sharing knowledge and influencing others through detailed insights and constructive feedback.

2. **The Validator**: Seeks to affirm the value of products or services through their experiences, providing authenticity and trust.

3. **The Collaborator**: Thrives in group settings and contributes to joint problem-solving and innovation.

4. **The Influencer**: Possesses a strong network and has the power to sway public opinion through their endorsements and critiques.

Engaging Personalities in Different Formats
Executive Advisory Boards (EABs)
- **Target Personality**: The Influencer, The Educator

- **Engagement Strategy**: EABs should focus on attracting Influencers and Educators who can provide high-level insights and drive consensus among top-tier executives. These members are invaluable for their ability to see the bigger picture and influence broader industry trends.

- **Best Practices**: Provide these personalities with data-driven discussions, strategic decision-making opportunities, and platforms to share their thought leadership.

Customer Advisory Boards (CABs)
- **Target Personality**: The Collaborator, The Validator

- **Engagement Strategy**: CABs benefit from Collaborators and Validators who can delve into specific product feedback and validate the practical use cases of your offerings.

- **Best Practices**: Foster an environment that encourages detailed feedback and shared experiences and organize breakout sessions that cater to their need for deep dives into product usage.

Co-Innovation Workstreams
- **Target Personality**: The Collaborator, The Educator

- **Engagement Strategy**: These sessions are ideal for Collaborators and Educators who can engage in creative problem-solving and provide expert insights to steer product development.

- **Best Practices**: Engage these personalities with hands-on activities, prototype testing, and collaborative workshops that leverage their expertise and creativity.

User Groups, Communities, and Meet-Ups

- **Target Personality**: The Educator, The Validator

- **Engagement Strategy**: User Groups should harness the energy of Educators and Validators to create a community-driven environment where users can learn from each other and validate new ideas.

- **Best Practices**: Regular meetups, Q&A sessions, and user-led presentations will keep these personalities engaged and active.

Customer References/Testimonials

- **Target Personality**: The Influencer, The Validator

- **Engagement Strategy**: For customer testimonials, Influencers and Validators are ideal as they provide credible endorsements and detailed accounts of their user experience, enhancing your brand's reliability.

- **Best Practices**: Create opportunities for them to share their success stories through various media, including case studies, video testimonials, and social media posts.

Conclusion

This detailed approach ensures that each customer engagement platform operates at its highest potential, leading to more successful outcomes and a stronger, more connected customer community.

Effectively engaging different customer personalities in appropriate formats not only enriches the experience for all involved but also significantly enhances the outcomes of customer engagement initiatives. By understanding and leveraging the unique strengths of these personalities, organizations can create more meaningful interactions and drive substantial business growth.

Key Takeaways

✓ Recognize and cater to specific customer personalities for different engagement formats.

- ✓ Tailor engagement strategies to maximize contributions and satisfaction of each personality type.
- ✓ Utilize diverse engagement platforms to harness the full spectrum of customer insights and advocacy.

9 Customer Engagement & Advocacy as part of the PYPR framework for Sustainable Product Success

Introduction

Mastering customer engagement and advocacy is pivotal in transforming every facet of your product's lifecycle and organizational impact. Within the PYPR framework, customer engagement and advocacy act as critical levers, enhancing each dimension of product success.

This chapter provides a detailed exploration of how these elements interact with the PYPR dimensions—Product Viability, Product Development, Go-to-Market/Product Marketing, The Market/Your Customers, Software Demonstrations and Training, and Organizational Maturity—to reinforce and amplify product success.

The various components of the Customer Advocacy Pyramid directly or indirectly influence every area of holistic product management, fostering a self-reinforcing cycle of continuous improvement and growth.

The Positive Cross-effects of Unleashing the Power of Customer Engagement & Advocacy

1. Product Viability: By providing early insights and fostering collaboration through CABs and co-innovation workstreams, customer engagement uncovers opportunities that enhance customer value, pipeline development, and profitability. Satisfied advocates also help expand market share through positive referrals, directly contributing to product growth. For example:

- **Customer Value & Pipeline Development:** Engagement through CABs and co-innovation workstreams facilitates early detection of market needs and product gaps, directly enhancing customer value and aiding in robust pipeline development.

- **Product Profitability & Growth:** Advocacy driven by deep customer engagement results in enhanced product adoption and expansion, significantly impacting profitability and market share.

2. Product Development: CABs and co-innovation groups offer invaluable feedback that refines your product vision and strategy while influencing roadmaps and product planning. Engaged customers actively participate in beta testing, quality assessments, and iterative feedback loops, helping your team deliver a well-executed product aligned with market needs. For example,

- **Vision, Strategy, and Roadmap Alignment:** Feedback from engaged customer groups ensures product developments are customer-centric, aligning closely with market demands and technological advancements.

- **Execution & Quality Assurance:** Regular interactions with customers during beta testing and feedback sessions contribute to a more refined product execution and enhance overall product quality.

3. Go-to-Market/Product Marketing: Leveraging customer communities, CAB members, and vibrant testimonials provide marketing assets that boost competitive analysis, empower sales teams, and strengthen partnerships. When customers share their success stories at industry events or through case studies, they amplify your message with unmatched authenticity. For example,

- **Market Positioning and Sales Enablement:** Utilizing testimonials and case studies in marketing materials not only boosts the brand's credibility but also equips the sales team with convincing narratives that resonate with prospective clients.

- **Partner Enablement & Competitive Analysis:** Engaged customers provide insights that help in fine-tuning competitive strategies and empowering channel partners with the right tools and knowledge.

4. The Market/Your Customers: Industry analysts and influencers take note when your product resonates deeply with its user base. Engaged advocates highlight thought leadership, functional completeness, and product quality while building a robust community of like-minded users and ensuring positive perceptions among the broader market. The "The Market / Your Customers" dimension is the center of Customer Engagement and Advocacy where this book and the application of the introduced concepts have most significant and direct impact. The success factors of Customer Community and Key Customer References & Support account for 40% of the overall weight within this key product success dimension, underscoring their critical role in driving peak performance. For example,

- **Building a Robust Customer Community:** Advocacy fosters a strong community, encouraging ongoing engagement and providing a platform for continuous customer feedback and support.

- **Influencer Relations & Thought Leadership:** Advocacy amplifies your company's voice in the market, establishing your brand as a thought leader while enhancing the perception of product quality and completeness through influential advocates.

5. Software Demonstrations and Training: Engaged customers become your best partners to understand real world usage of your products and the value you are providing. These usage-based insights inform tailored product demonstrations, improving pre-sales enablement and overall quality. For example,

- **Enhanced Training Materials & Pre-Sales Enablement:** Engaged users often produce real-world use cases and scenarios that enhance training materials, making demonstrations more relevant and impactful.

6. Organizational Maturity: Customer advocacy fosters a product-focused mindset across the organization. It encourages a structure where each team member understands the importance of customer value and embodies a culture of continuous improvement. This drives alignment between leadership, vision, and team collaboration.

- **Cultural Shift Towards Customer-Centricity:** Advocacy encourages a culture of customer focus across the organization, aligning product teams and leadership with the core values of customer satisfaction and engagement.

- **Strategic Alignment & Improved Processes:** Feedback from engaged customers influences strategic decisions, helping refine internal processes and align them more closely with market needs.

The Role of Advocacy in Amplifying Impact

Customer advocacy not only enhances direct interactions with products but also serves as a force multiplier across organizational functions. Advocates help reduce customer acquisition costs by acting as organic marketers and enhance customer lifetime value through increased loyalty and reduced churn. Their insights lead to products that not only meet but exceed market expectations, thereby boosting overall company valuation.

Conclusion

This chapter underlines the indispensable role of customer engagement and advocacy within the PYPR framework, illustrating how they permeate and enhance every aspect of holistic product management. By integrating customer insights into all facets of product strategy and execution, organizations can achieve a sustainable competitive advantage, resulting in products that are not only successful in the market but also cherished by users and customers.

To truly succeed in today's competitive landscape, embracing a holistic approach to product management—powered by a strong foundation of customer engagement and advocacy—is essential. This approach ensures that all aspects of product management are aligned to effectively leverage customer insights for continuous growth and improvement.

Explore More Resources

Are you inspired to dive deeper into holistic product management? There's a wealth of resources waiting for you! Whether you're seeking to expand your knowledge or implement the practices discussed, here are several avenues to explore:

- **Discover the Comprehensive PYPR Book**: Delve deeper into the nuances of holistic product management and the Product Yield

Potential Radar framework to unlock your product's full potential. Find it on Amazon.

- **Product&360 Nugget Series**: Continue your journey with our series, which offers focused insights and tools for reaching peak performance in product management. Explore the series [here: https://www.productand.com/product-360-nuggets-series](https://www.productand.com/product-360-nuggets-series).

- **Visit the Product& Homepage**: For more resources, including testimonials, workshops, assessments, and coaching options, visit [Product& at https://www.productand.com/](https://www.productand.com/).

- **Access Our Toolkit**: Implement what you've learned with practical tools and templates from our Holistic Product Management Toolkit.

Your product and your team deserve the best tools and strategies to achieve peak performance. Engage with these resources to ensure your product efforts lead to real and lasting success.

About the Author

For over two decades, Timo has been leading product organizations and spearheading exceptional enterprise and consumer products with teams across the globe at industry giants like Google, SAP, and CAS.

Currently Timo guides product teams as a Product Lead, Commerce at Google. Prior to Google, Timo had the role of Global VP of Product Management at SAP. As Head of Product, he shaped and drove multiple 0 to 1 product successes that address market needs all the way to delivering value for customers and SAP. He started his product career as the first product manager reporting directly to the CTO and start-up co-founder at CAS, where he scaled and established product management supporting the company's growth journey. Timo gained his experience working in organizations that range from 30 employees to more than 180.000 employees.

As the founder of Product&, Timo supports clients in elevating product organizations and products to their peak potential. Through customized workshops and precise 360 assessments, he equips clients with the tools they need for success.

Connect:

References

Gadam, S. (24. April 2024). *What is a customer advisory board? Best practices, agenda, benefits*. Von logrocket.com: https://blog.logrocket.com/product-management/customer-advisory-board-best-practices-agenda/ abgerufen

How To Create Customer Advisory Boards That Deliver Value. (2. May 2024). Von satrixsolutions.com: https://www.satrixsolutions.com/blog/how-to-create-customer-advisory-boards-that-deliver-value abgerufen

Jensen, R. (2017). Von pragmatic-marketing: https://cdn.agilitycms.com/pragmatic-marketing-v2/pdf/PRAGMATICMARKETERSUMMER2017.pdf abgerufen

Klein, E. (30. April 2024). *Setting The Customer Advisory Board Meeting Agenda*. Von satrixsolutions.com: https://www.satrixsolutions.com/blog/setting-the-customer-advisory-board-meeting-agenda abgerufen

Klein, E. (1. May 2024). *The Customer Advisory Board Invitation Letter*. Von satrixsolutions.com: https://www.satrixsolutions.com/blog/the-customer-advisory-board-invitation-letter abgerufen

McCloskey, H. (6. May 2024). *How to Start a Customer Advisory Board*. Von uservoice.com: https://www.uservoice.com/blog/cab-best-practices abgerufen

Meabe, C. (18. May 2024). *Foundation Inc*. Von foundationinc.co: https://foundationinc.co/lab/miro-templates/ abgerufen

Nathan, G. (3. May 2024). *10 Reasons to Serve on Customer Advisory Boards*. Von customeradvisoryboard.org: https://customeradvisoryboard.org/best-practices/serve-on-customer-advisory-boards/ abgerufen

Ramos, L. (18. Jan 2024). *Forrester*. Von forrester.com: https://www.forrester.com/blogs/four-advocate-personalities-turn-customer-goodwill-into-gold/ abgerufen

Ramos, L. (23. Feb 2024). *Modern (B2B) Love: Deepen Customer Relationships With Post-Sale Engagement Marketing*. Von forrester.com: https://www.forrester.com/blogs/modern-b2b-love-deepen-customer-relationships-with-post-sale-engagement-marketing/ abgerufen

Urban, G. L. (1. May 2024). *Customer Advocacy: A New Era in Marketing?* Von https://citeseerx.ist.psu.edu/: https://citeseerx.ist.psu.edu/document?repid=rep1&type=pdf&doi=ab242ecd23a6497130327e1cc05779bc860c1139 abgerufen

Figures

FIGURE 1: B2B PRODUCT PYPR BLUEPRINT 16
FIGURE 2: THE ENGAGEMENT-ADVOCACY FLYWHEEL...21
FIGURE 3: THE CUSTOMER ADVOCACY PYRAMID 34
FIGURE 4: THE ENGAGEMENT-ADVOCACY FLYWHEEL IN ACTION 42
FIGURE 5: 5-STEP CUSTOMER ADVISORY BOARD RECIPE 50
FIGURE 6: HIGH-LEVEL CAB TIMELINE 55
FIGURE 7: THE CUSTOMER ADVOCACY PYRAMID 86

www.ingramcontent.com/pod-product-compliance
Lightning Source LLC
Chambersburg PA
CBHW071212240526
45470CB00018B/1775